I Have, Who Has?

MATH

1–2

Written by
Trisha Callella

Editor: Jennifer Busby
Cover Illustrator: Priscilla Burris
Production: Carlie Hayashi
Cover Designer: Barbara Peterson
Art Director: Moonhee Pak
Managing Editor: Betsy Morris, Ph.D.

Table of Contents

Introduction

I HAVE, WHO HAS? is a series of books that provide reinforcement with various academic skills through an interactive group activity. The activities consist of game cards that students read and interactively answer. Each game also features an active listening enrichment activity. This component gives students additional practice in auditory discrimination and extends their learning to the application level.

I Have, Who Has? Math 1–2 provides a fun, interactive way for students to practice various math skills. It includes 37 card games that will help improve students' listening skills and reinforce standards-based math skills. A blank reproducible card template and a blank reproducible active listening enrichment activity page are provided to allow you to create your own I Have, Who Has? card game. The skills addressed in this resource include the following:

- Addition
- Subtraction
- Fact families
- More than, less than
- Number patterns
- Place value

- Time
- Money
- Measurement
- Data analysis
- Problem solving
- Algebra

The ease and simplicity of preparing these games for your class will allow you to begin using *I Have, Who Has?* today! These engaging games are sure to keep students involved as they learn valuable math skills.

ORGANIZATION

Each card game consists of 32 question and answer cards. The cards are arranged in columns (top to bottom) in the order they will be read by the class. A reproducible active listening enrichment page follows each set of game cards. Play the interactive card games by themselves or in conjunction with this reproducible page to reinforce students' active listening, increase active participation, provide enrichment, and extend and transfer the learning and accountability of each child.

INSTRUCTIONS FOR I HAVE, WHO HAS GAME CARDS

1) Photocopy two sets of the game cards. Keep one copy as your reference to the correct order of the questions and answers.

2) Cut apart the second set of game cards. Mix up the cards and pass them out to the students. Every student should have at least one card. Depending on your class size, students may have more than one card.

3) Have the student with the first card begin the game by saying *I have the first card. Who has…?* As each student reads a card, monitor your copy to make sure students are reading the cards in the correct order. If students correctly matched each card, then the last card read will "loop" back to the first card and read *I have…Who has the first card?*

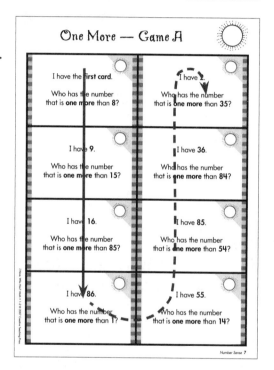

INSTRUCTIONS FOR ACTIVE LISTENING ENRICHMENT PAGE

1) This page is optional and is not necessary to play the game.

2) Copy one page for each student or pair of students.

3) Make sure each student has a light-colored crayon or highlighter (not a marker or pencil) to color in the correct boxes as they are read.

4) After the last card is read, have students answer the extension questions at the bottom of the page. Use the answer key on pages 198–208 to check students' answers.

5) Some games require an overhead transparency. For those activities, copy the reproducible on an overhead transparency. Display the transparency as students play the game.

WHAT TO OBSERVE

1) Students who have difficulty locating the correct boxes on the active listening enrichment page, once familiar with the game format, may have difficulties with visual discrimination.

2) Students who have difficulty reading their card at the correct time may have difficulties with attention, hearing, active listening, or the concepts being reinforced.

VARIATIONS
(To be played without the active listening enrichment page)

Timed Version
Have students play the game twice. Encourage them to beat their time in the second round. Have students play the same game again the next day. Can they beat their time again? Remember to mix up the cards before distributing them for each new game.

Small Groups
Give each group a set of game cards. Encourage groups to pay close attention, read quickly, and stay on task to determine which group is the fastest. Playing in smaller groups allows students to have more cards. This raises the opportunity for individual accountability, active participation, time on task, and reinforcement per child.

Card Reduction
If your class is not ready to play with multiple cards, you can reduce the number to fit your class needs. Photocopy the set of the cards you want to play. Determine the appropriate number of cards needed. Following the existing order of the game, begin with the first card and count the number of cards you need. Delete the *Who Has...?* clue from the last card counted and replace with the sentence *Who has the first card?* Photocopy and cut apart the revised game for class play.

One More — Game A

I have the **first card**.

Who has the number
that is **one more** than 8?

I have **2**.

Who has the number
that is **one more** than 35?

I have **9**.

Who has the number
that is **one more** than 15?

I have **36**.

Who has the number
that is **one more** than 84?

I have **16**.

Who has the number
that is **one more** than 85?

I have **85**.

Who has the number
that is **one more** than 54?

I have **86**.

Who has the number
that is **one more** than 1?

I have **55**.

Who has the number
that is **one more** than 14?

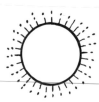

One More — Game A

I have **15**.

Who has the number
that is **one more** than **91**?

I have **35**.

Who has the number
that is **one more** than **10**?

I have **92**.

Who has the number
that is **one more** than **21**?

I have **11**.

Who has the number
that is **one more** than **80**?

I have **22**.

Who has the number
that is **one more** than **55**?

I have **81**.

Who has the number
that is **one more** than **89**?

I have **56**.

Who has the number
that is **one more** than **34**?

I have **90**.

Who has the number
that is **one more** than **19**?

I Have, Who Has?: Math • 1–2 © 2007 Creative Teaching Press

One More — Game A

I have **20**.

Who has the number
that is **one more** than **28**?

I have **95**.

Who has the number
that is **one more** than **12**?

I have **29**.

Who has the number
that is **one more** than **42**?

I have **13**.

Who has the number
that is **one more** than **78**?

I have **43**.

Who has the number
that is **one more** than **47**?

I have **79**.

Who has the number
that is **one more** than **82**?

I have **48**.

Who has the number
that is **one more** than **94**?

I have **83**.

Who has the number
that is **one more** than **17**?

One More — Game A

I have **18**.

Who has the number
that is **one more** than **50**?

I have **96**.

Who has the number
that is **one more** than **87**?

I have **51**.

Who has the number
that is **one more** than **59**?

I have **88**.

Who has the number
that is **one more** than **51**?

I have **60**.

Who has the number
that is **one more** than **71**?

I have **52**.

Who has the number
that is **one more** than **58**?

I have **72**.

Who has the number
that is **one more** than **95**?

I have **59**.

Who has the **first card**?

I Have, Who Has?: Math • 1–2 © 2007 Creative Teaching Press

Name _____ Date _____

One More — Game A

I Lightly color each number that matches your classmates' answers.

1	2	3	4	5	6	7	8	9	10
11	12	13	14	15	16	17	18	19	20
21	22	23	24	25	26	27	28	29	30
31	32	33	34	35	36	37	38	39	40
41	42	43	44	45	46	47	48	49	50
51	52	53	54	55	56	57	58	59	60
61	62	63	64	65	66	67	68	69	70
71	72	73	74	75	76	77	78	79	80
81	82	83	84	85	86	87	88	89	90
91	92	93	94	95	96	97	98	99	100

II Choose 10 numbers from the hundred chart that you did **not** color. Write the numbers in the chart below. Rewrite **each** number as **one more**.

Number from the 100 Chart										
One More										

One More — Game B

I have the **first card**. Who has the number that is **one more** than **110**?	I have **171**. Who has the number that is **one more** than **109**?
I have **111**. Who has the number that is **one more** than **115**?	I have **110**. Who has the number that is **one more** than **189**?
I have **116**. Who has the number that is **one more** than **154**?	I have **190**. Who has the number that is **one more** than **112**?
I have **155**. Who has the number that is **one more** than **170**?	I have **113**. Who has the number that is **one more** than **149**?

I Have, Who Has?: Math • 1–2 © 2007 Creative Teaching Press

One More — Game B

I have **150**.

Who has the number
that is **one more** than **187**?

I have **174**.

Who has the number
that is **one more** than **180**?

I have **188**.

Who has the number
that is **one more** than **190**?

I have **181**.

Who has the number
that is **one more** than **184**?

I have **191**.

Who has the number
that is **one more** than **159**?

I have **185**.

Who has the number
that is **one more** than **114**?

I have **160**.

Who has the number
that is **one more** than **173**?

I have **115**.

Who has the number
that is **one more** than **129**?

I have **130**.

Who has the number
that is **one more** than **136**?

I have **200**.

Who has the number
that is **one more** than **202**?

I have **137**.

Who has the number
that is **one more** than **169**?

I have **203**.

Who has the number
that is **one more** than **299**?

I have **170**.

Who has the number
that is **one more** than **161**?

I have **300**.

Who has the number
that is **one more** than **217**?

I have **162**.

Who has the number
that is **one more** than **199**?

I have **218**.

Who has the number
that is **one more** than **239**?

One More — Game B

I have **240**.

Who has the number
that is **one more** than **250**?

I have **212**.

Who has the number
that is **one more** than **209**?

I have **251**.

Who has the number
that is **one more** than **268**?

I have **210**.

Who has the number
that is **one more** than **251**?

I have **269**.

Who has the number
that is **one more** than **279**?

I have **252**.

Who has the number
that is **one more** than **207**?

I have **280**.

Who has the number
that is **one more** than **211**?

I have **208**.

Who has the **first card**?

One More — Game B

I Write each number from left to right as your classmates say the answers.

*Start →							

II Choose 12 numbers from the chart above. Write the numbers in the chart below. Rewrite **each** number as **one more**.

Number from the Chart	One More	Number from the Chart	One More

One Less — Game A

I have the **first card**.

Who has the number
that is **one less** than **11**?

I have **66**.

Who has the number
that is **one less** than **56**?

I have **10**.

Who has the number
that is **one less** than **91**?

I have **55**.

Who has the number
that is **one less** than **82**?

I have **90**.

Who has the number
that is **one less** than **36**?

I have **81**.

Who has the number
that is **one less** than **23**?

I have **35**.

Who has the number
that is **one less** than **67**?

I have **22**.

Who has the number
that is **one less** than **30**?

One Less — Game A

I have **29**.

Who has the number that is **one less** than **47**?

I have **20**.

Who has the number that is **one less** than **87**?

I have **46**.

Who has the number that is **one less** than **7**?

I have **86**.

Who has the number that is **one less** than **16**?

I have **6**.

Who has the number that is **one less** than **96**?

I have **15**.

Who has the number that is **one less** than **76**?

I have **95**.

Who has the number that is **one less** than **21**?

I have **75**.

Who has the number that is **one less** than **73**?

One Less — Game A

I have **72**.

Who has the number
that is **one less** than **80**?

I have **40**.

Who has the number
that is **one less** than **71**?

I have **79**.

Who has the number
that is **one less** than **93**?

I have **70**.

Who has the number
that is **one less** than **62**?

I have **92**.

Who has the number
that is **one less** than **3**?

I have **61**.

Who has the number
that is **one less** than **32**?

I have **2**.

Who has the number
that is **one less** than **41**?

I have **31**.

Who has the number
that is **one less** than **27**?

One Less — Game A

I have **26**.

Who has the number that is **one less** than 10?

I have **57**.

Who has the number that is **one less** than 55?

I have **9**.

Who has the number that is **one less** than 100?

I have **54**.

Who has the number that is **one less** than 48?

I have **99**.

Who has the number that is **one less** than 45?

I have **47**.

Who has the number that is **one less** than 61?

I have **44**.

Who has the number that is **one less** than 58?

I have **60**.

Who has the **first card**?

I Have, Who Has?: Math • 1–2 © 2007 Creative Teaching Press

Name _____ Date _____

One Less — Game A

I Lightly color each number that matches your classmates' answers.

1	2	3	4	5	6	7	8	9	10
11	12	13	14	15	16	17	18	19	20
21	22	23	24	25	26	27	28	29	30
31	32	33	34	35	36	37	38	39	40
41	42	43	44	45	46	47	48	49	50
51	52	53	54	55	56	57	58	59	60
61	62	63	64	65	66	67	68	69	70
71	72	73	74	75	76	77	78	79	80
81	82	83	84	85	86	87	88	89	90
91	92	93	94	95	96	97	98	99	100

II Choose 10 numbers from the hundred chart that you did **not** color. Write the numbers in the chart below. Rewrite **each** number as **one less**.

Number from the 100 Chart										
One Less										

I Have, Who Has?: Math • 1–2 © 2007 Creative Teaching Press

One Less — Game B

I have the **first card**.

Who has the number
that is **one less** than 102?

I have **120**.

Who has the number
that is **one less** than 158?

I have **101**.

Who has the number
that is **one less** than 150?

I have **157**.

Who has the number
that is **one less** than 166?

I have **149**.

Who has the number
that is **one less** than 115?

I have **165**.

Who has the number
that is **one less** than 180?

I have **114**.

Who has the number
that is **one less** than 121?

I have **179**.

Who has the number
that is **one less** than 191?

One Less — Game B

I have **190**.

Who has the number
that is **one less** than **200**?

I have **249**.

Who has the number
that is **one less** than **266**?

I have **199**.

Who has the number
that is **one less** than **112**?

I have **265**.

Who has the number
that is **one less** than **281**?

I have **111**.

Who has the number
that is **one less** than **194**?

I have **280**.

Who has the number
that is **one less** than **290**?

I have **193**.

Who has the number
that is **one less** than **250**?

I have **289**.

Who has the number
that is **one less** than **215**?

One Less — Game B

I have **214**.

Who has the number
that is **one less** than **210**?

I have **299**.

Who has the number
that is **one less** than **305**?

I have **209**.

Who has the number
that is **one less** than **283**?

I have **304**.

Who has the number
that is **one less** than **320**?

I have **282**.

Who has the number
that is **one less** than **279**?

I have **319**.

Who has the number
that is **one less** than **355**?

I have **278**.

Who has the number
that is **one less** than **300**?

I have **354**.

Who has the number
that is **one less** than **371**?

One Less — Game B

I have **370**.

Who has the number
that is **one less** than **389**?

I have **359**.

Who has the number
that is **one less** than **364**?

I have **388**.

Who has the number
that is **one less** than **321**?

I have **363**.

Who has the number
that is **one less** than **400**?

I have **320**.

Who has the number
that is **one less** than **399**?

I have **399**.

Who has the number
that is **one less** than **401**?

I have **398**.

Who has the number
that is **one less** than **360**?

I have **400**.

Who has the **first card**?

One Less — Game B

I Finish the maze by lightly coloring the answers as your classmates say them.

*Start	101	149	154	249	265	302	400	*Finish
157	120	114	111	193	280	360	399	489
165	179	190	199	500	289	359	363	470
100	200	278	282	209	214	398	396	220
420	305	299	354	370	388	320	290	313
340	320	304	319	378	312	404	331	428

II Choose 20 numbers that you did **not** color in the maze above. Write the numbers in the charts below. Rewrite the number as **one less**.

Number from the Maze									
One Less									

Number from the Maze									
One Less									

I Have, Who Has?: Math • 1–2 © 2007 Creative Teaching Press

One More, One Less Review

I have the **first card**.

Who has the number
that is **one more** than 24?

I have **20**.

Who has the number
that is **one more** than 10?

I have **25**.

Who has the number
that is **one less** than 17?

I have **11**.

Who has the number
that is **one less** than 30?

I have **16**.

Who has the number
that is **one less** than 31?

I have **29**.

Who has the number
that is **one less** than 45?

I have **30**.

Who has the number
that is **one more** than 19?

I have **44**.

Who has the number
that is **one more** than 20?

One More, One Less Review

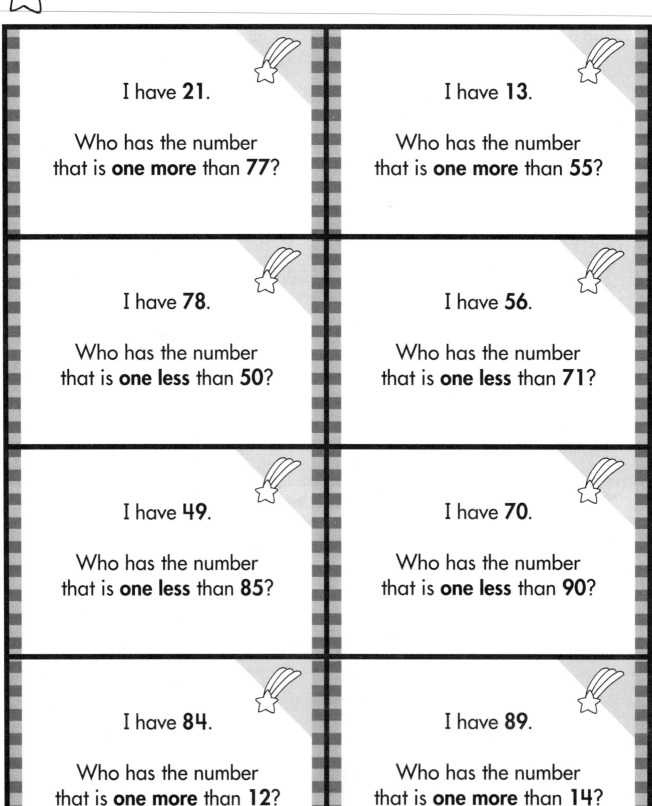

I have **21**.

Who has the number
that is **one more** than **77**?

I have **13**.

Who has the number
that is **one more** than **55**?

I have **78**.

Who has the number
that is **one less** than **50**?

I have **56**.

Who has the number
that is **one less** than **71**?

I have **49**.

Who has the number
that is **one less** than **85**?

I have **70**.

Who has the number
that is **one less** than **90**?

I have **84**.

Who has the number
that is **one more** than **12**?

I have **89**.

Who has the number
that is **one more** than **14**?

I Have, Who Has?: Math • 1–2 © 2007 Creative Teaching Press

One More, One Less Review

I have **15**.

Who has the number
that is **one more** than 66?

I have **91**.

Who has the number
that is **one more** than 50?

I have **67**.

Who has the number
that is **one less** than 63?

I have **51**.

Who has the number
that is **one less** than 60?

I have **62**.

Who has the number
that is **one less** than 76?

I have **59**.

Who has the number
that is **one less** than 37?

I have **75**.

Who has the number
that is **one more** than 90?

I have **36**.

Who has the number
that is **one more** than 17?

One More, One Less Review

I have **18**.

Who has the number that is **one more** than **79**?

I have **48**.

Who has the number that is **one more** than **41**?

I have **80**.

Who has the number that is **one less** than **70**?

I have **42**.

Who has the number that is **one less** than **20**?

I have **69**.

Who has the number that is **one less** than **40**?

I have **19**.

Who has the number that is **one less** than **88**?

I have **39**.

Who has the number that is **one more** than **47**?

I have **87**.

Who has the **first card**?

I Have, Who Has?: Math • 1–2 © 2007 Creative Teaching Press

Name _____ Date _____

One More, One Less Review

I Write each number from left to right as your classmates say the answers.

*Start →							

II Choose 10 numbers from the chart above. Write the numbers in the charts below. Rewrite each number as **one less** and **one more**. The first one has been done for you.

One Less	Number from the Chart	One More
47	48	49

One Less	Number from the Chart	One More

I Have, Who Has? Math • 1–2 © 2007 Creative Teaching Press

Two More, Five More

I have the **first card**.

Who has the number
that is **two more** than 8?

I have **25**.

Who has the number
that is **five more** than 10?

I have **10**.

Who has the number
that is **two more** than 20?

I have **15**.

Who has the number
that is **two more** than 3?

I have **22**.

Who has the number
that is **two more** than 15?

I have **5**.

Who has the number
that is **two more** than 30?

I have **17**.

Who has the number
that is **five more** than 20?

I have **32**.

Who has the number
that is **five more** than 40?

I Have, Who Has?: Math • 1–2 © 2007 Creative Teaching Press

Two More, Five More

I have **45**.

Who has the number
that is **five more** than **15**?

I have **36**.

Who has the number
that is **two more** than **42**?

I have **20**.

Who has the number
that is **five more** than **45**?

I have **44**.

Who has the number
that is **five more** than **30**?

I have **50**.

Who has the number
that is **two more** than **1**?

I have **35**.

Who has the number
that is **five more** than **35**?

I have **3**.

Who has the number
that is **two more** than **34**?

I have **40**.

Who has the number
that is **two more** than **16**?

Two More, Five More

I have **18**.

Who has the number
that is **two more** than **40**?

I have **26**.

Who has the number
that is **five more** than **41**?

I have **42**.

Who has the number
that is **two more** than **11**?

I have **46**.

Who has the number
that is **five more** than **1**?

I have **13**.

Who has the number
that is **five more** than **25**?

I have **6**.

Who has the number
that is **two more** than **10**?

I have **30**.

Who has the number
that is **five more** than **21**?

I have **12**.

Who has the number
that is **five more** than **11**?

Two More, Five More

I have **16**.

Who has the number
that is **two more** than **45**?

I have **41**.

Who has the number
that is **five more** than **4**?

I have **47**.

Who has the number
that is **two more** than **0**?

I have **9**.

Who has the number
that is **two more** than **9**?

I have **2**.

Who has the number
that is **two more** than **19**?

I have **11**.

Who has the number
that is **two more** than **29**?

I have **21**.

Who has the number
that is **two more** than **39**?

I have **31**.

Who has the **first card**?

I Have, Who Has? Math • 1–2 © 2007 Creative Teaching Press

Name _____ Date _____

Two More, Five More

I Write each number from left to right as your classmates say the answers.

*Start →							

II Choose 11 numbers from the chart above. Write the numbers in the chart below. Rewrite each number as **two more** and **five more**. The first one has been done for you.

Number from the Chart	Two More	Five More
10	12	15

I Have, Who Has?: Math • 1–2 © 2007 Creative Teaching Press

Two Less, Five Less

I have the **first card**.

Who has the number that is **five less** than **10**?

I have **15**.

Who has the number that is **five less** than **35**?

I have **5**.

Who has the number that is **five less** than **25**?

I have **30**.

Who has the number that is **five less** than **18**?

I have **20**.

Who has the number that is **two less** than **10**?

I have **13**.

Who has the number that is **two less** than **50**?

I have **8**.

Who has the number that is **two less** than **17**?

I have **48**.

Who has the number that is **two less** than **6**?

Two Less, Five Less

I have **4**.

Who has the number that is **five less** than **40**?

I have **25**.

Who has the number that is **five less** than **5**?

I have **35**.

Who has the number that is **five less** than **45**?

I have **0**.

Who has the number that is **five less** than **19**?

I have **40**.

Who has the number that is **two less** than **4**?

I have **14**.

Who has the number that is **two less** than **38**?

I have **2**.

Who has the number that is **two less** than **27**?

I have **36**.

Who has the number that is **two less** than **47**?

I Have, Who Has?: Math • 1–2 © 2007 Creative Teaching Press

Two Less, Five Less

I have **45**.

Who has the number
that is **five less** than **15**?

I have **38**.

Who has the number
that is **five less** than **11**?

I have **10**.

Who has the number
that is **five less** than **55**?

I have **6**.

Who has the number
that is **five less** than **47**?

I have **50**.

Who has the number
that is **two less** than **20**?

I have **42**.

Who has the number
that is **two less** than **30**?

I have **18**.

Who has the number
that is **two less** than **40**?

I have **28**.

Who has the number
that is **two less** than **21**?

Two Less, Five Less

I have **19**.

Who has the number that is **five less** than **46**?

I have **11**.

Who has the number that is **five less** than **12**?

I have **41**.

Who has the number that is **five less** than **27**?

I have **7**.

Who has the number that is **five less** than **21**?

I have **22**.

Who has the number that is **two less** than **25**?

I have **16**.

Who has the number that is **two less** than **31**?

I have **23**.

Who has the number that is **two less** than **13**?

I have **29**.

Who has the **first card**?

I Have, Who Has?: Math • 1–2 © 2007 Creative Teaching Press

Two Less, Five Less

I Finish the maze by lightly coloring the answers as your classmates say them.

*Start	5	45	10	50	18	38	81
95	20	36	14	12	3	6	42
15	8	35	0	80	75	19	28
30	13	45	25	23	22	41	66
51	48	4	2	11	64	70	52
73	62	35	40	7	16	29	*Finish

II Choose 8 numbers that you did **not** color in the maze. Write the numbers in the chart below. Rewrite each number as **two less** and **five less**. The first one has been done for you.

Number from the Maze	Two Less	Five Less
73	71	68

Ten More — Game A

I have the **first card**.

Who has the number
that is **ten more** than 15?

I have **75**.

Who has the number
that is **ten more** than 6?

I have **25**.

Who has the number
that is **ten more** than 80?

I have **16**.

Who has the number
that is **ten more** than 76?

I have **90**.

Who has the number
that is **ten more** than 20?

I have **86**.

Who has the number
that is **ten more** than 5?

I have **30**.

Who has the number
that is **ten more** than 65?

I have **15**.

Who has the number
that is **ten more** than 11?

I Have, Who Has?: Math • 1–2 © 2007 Creative Teaching Press

Ten More — Game A

I have **21**.

Who has the number
that is **ten more** than **71**?

I have **85**.

Who has the number
that is **ten more** than **1**?

I have **81**.

Who has the number
that is **ten more** than **66**?

I have **11**.

Who has the number
that is **ten more** than **70**?

I have **76**.

Who has the number
that is **ten more** than **16**?

I have **80**.

Who has the number
that is **ten more** than **61**?

I have **26**.

Who has the number
that is **ten more** than **75**?

I have **71**.

Who has the number
that is **ten more** than **27**?

Ten More — Game A

I have **37**.

Who has the number
that is **ten more** than **52**?

I have **54**.

Who has the number
that is **ten more** than **57**?

I have **62**.

Who has the number
that is **ten more** than **59**?

I have **67**.

Who has the number
that is **ten more** than **29**?

I have **69**.

Who has the number
that is **ten more** than **22**?

I have **39**.

Who has the number
that is **ten more** than **47**?

I have **32**.

Who has the number
that is **ten more** than **44**?

I have **57**.

Who has the number
that is **ten more** than **54**?

I Have, Who Has?: Math • 1–2 © 2007 Creative Teaching Press

Ten More — Game A

I have **64**.

Who has the number
that is **ten more** than **24**?

I have **28**.

Who has the number
that is **ten more** than **63**?

I have **34**.

Who has the number
that is **ten more** than **68**?

I have **73**.

Who has the number
that is **ten more** than **82**?

I have **78**.

Who has the number
that is **ten more** than **13**?

I have **92**.

Who has the number
that is **ten more** than **89**?

I have **23**.

Who has the number
that is **ten more** than **18**?

I have **99**.

Who has the **first card**?

I Have, Who Has?: Math • 1–2 © 2007 Creative Teaching Press

Ten More — Game A

I Lightly color each number that matches your classmates' answers.

1	2	3	4	5	6	7	8	9	10
11	12	13	14	15	16	17	18	19	20
21	22	23	24	25	26	27	28	29	30
31	32	33	34	35	36	37	38	39	40
41	42	43	44	45	46	47	48	49	50
51	52	53	54	55	56	57	58	59	60
61	62	63	64	65	66	67	68	69	70
71	72	73	74	75	76	77	78	79	80
81	82	83	84	85	86	87	88	89	90
91	92	93	94	95	96	97	98	99	100

II Choose 10 numbers from the hundred chart that you did **not** color. Write the numbers in the chart below. Rewrite **each** number as **ten more**.

Number from the 100 Chart										
Ten More										

I Have, Who Has?: Math • 1–2 © 2007 Creative Teaching Press

Ten More — Game B

I have the **first card**.

Who has the number
that is **ten more** than **100**?

I have **107**.

Who has the number
that is **ten more** than **114**?

I have **110**.

Who has the number
that is **ten more** than **105**?

I have **124**.

Who has the number
that is **ten more** than **91**?

I have **115**.

Who has the number
that is **ten more** than **120**?

I have **101**.

Who has the number
that is **ten more** than **122**?

I have **130**.

Who has the number
that is **ten more** than **97**?

I have **132**.

Who has the number
that is **ten more** than **133**?

I have **143**.

Who has the number
that is **ten more** than **149**?

I have **103**.

Who has the number
that is **ten more** than **111**?

I have **159**.

Who has the number
that is **ten more** than **180**?

I have **121**.

Who has the number
that is **ten more** than **117**?

I have **190**.

Who has the number
that is **ten more** than **177**?

I have **127**.

Who has the number
that is **ten more** than **96**?

I have **187**.

Who has the number
that is **ten more** than **93**?

I have **106**.

Who has the number
that is **ten more** than **116**?

I Have, Who Has?: Math • 1–2 © 2007 Creative Teaching Press

Ten More — Game B

I have **126**.

Who has the number
that is **ten more** than **189**?

I have **204**.

Who has the number
that is **ten more** than **210**?

I have **199**.

Who has the number
that is **ten more** than **171**?

I have **220**.

Who has the number
that is **ten more** than **255**?

I have **181**.

Who has the number
that is **ten more** than **190**?

I have **265**.

Who has the number
that is **ten more** than **191**?

I have **200**.

Who has the number
that is **ten more** than **194**?

I have **201**.

Who has the number
that is **ten more** than **199**?

I have **209**.

Who has the number
that is **ten more** than **214**?

I have **208**.

Who has the number
that is **ten more** than **203**?

I have **224**.

Who has the number
that is **ten more** than **276**?

I have **213**.

Who has the number
that is **ten more** than **295**?

I have **286**.

Who has the number
that is **ten more** than **289**?

I have **305**.

Who has the number
that is **ten more** than **310**?

I have **299**.

Who has the number
that is **ten more** than **198**?

I have **320**.

Who has the **first card**?

I Have, Who Has?: Math • 1–2 © 2007 Creative Teaching Press

Name _____ Date _____

Ten More — Game B

I Write each number from left to right as your classmates say the answers.

*Start →						

II Choose 12 numbers from the chart above. Write the numbers in the charts below. Rewrite **each** number as **ten more**.

Number from the Chart	Ten More

Number from the Chart	Ten More

Ten Less — Game A

I have the **first card**.

Who has the number that is **ten less** than **20**?

I have **78**.

Who has the number that is **ten less** than **95**?

I have **10**.

Who has the number that is **ten less** than **36**?

I have **85**.

Who has the number that is **ten less** than **92**?

I have **26**.

Who has the number that is **ten less** than **65**?

I have **82**.

Who has the number that is **ten less** than **11**?

I have **55**.

Who has the number that is **ten less** than **88**?

I have **1**.

Who has the number that is **ten less** than **15**?

I Have, Who Has?: Math • 1–2 © 2007 Creative Teaching Press

Ten Less — Game A

I have **5**.

Who has the number
that is **ten less** than 44?

I have **46**.

Who has the number
that is **ten less** than 22?

I have **34**.

Who has the number
that is **ten less** than 75?

I have **12**.

Who has the number
that is **ten less** than 29?

I have **65**.

Who has the number
that is **ten less** than 77?

I have **19**.

Who has the number
that is **ten less** than 16?

I have **67**.

Who has the number
that is **ten less** than 56?

I have **6**.

Who has the number
that is **ten less** than 33?

I have **23**.

Who has the number
that is **ten less** than **74**?

I have **37**.

Who has the number
that is **ten less** than **26**?

I have **64**.

Who has the number
that is **ten less** than **86**?

I have **16**.

Who has the number
that is **ten less** than **61**?

I have **76**.

Who has the number
that is **ten less** than **35**?

I have **51**.

Who has the number
that is **ten less** than **70**?

I have **25**.

Who has the number
that is **ten less** than **47**?

I have **60**.

Who has the number
that is **ten less** than **66**?

I Have, Who Has?: Math • 1–2 © 2007 Creative Teaching Press

Ten Less — Game A

I have **56**.

Who has the number
that is **ten less** than **55**?

I have **73**.

Who has the number
that is **ten less** than **99**?

I have **45**.

Who has the number
that is **ten less** than **96**?

I have **89**.

Who has the number
that is **ten less** than **38**?

I have **86**.

Who has the number
that is **ten less** than **85**?

I have **28**.

Who has the number
that is **ten less** than **76**?

I have **75**.

Who has the number
that is **ten less** than **83**?

I have **66**.

Who has the **first card**?

Ten Less — Game A

I Lightly color each number that matches your classmates' answers.

1	2	3	4	5	6	7	8	9	10
11	12	13	14	15	16	17	18	19	20
21	22	23	24	25	26	27	28	29	30
31	32	33	34	35	36	37	38	39	40
41	42	43	44	45	46	47	48	49	50
51	52	53	54	55	56	57	58	59	60
61	62	63	64	65	66	67	68	69	70
71	72	73	74	75	76	77	78	79	80
81	82	83	84	85	86	87	88	89	90
91	92	93	94	95	96	97	98	99	100

II Choose 10 numbers from the hundred chart that you did **not** color. Write the numbers in the chart below. Rewrite **each** number as **ten less**.

Number from the 100 Chart										
Ten Less										

I Have, Who Has?: Math • 1–2 © 2007 Creative Teaching Press

Ten Less — Game B

I have the **first card**.

Who has the number
that is **ten less** than **111**?

I have **127**.

Who has the number
that is **ten less** than **144**?

I have **101**.

Who has the number
that is **ten less** than **115**?

I have **134**.

Who has the number
that is **ten less** than **199**?

I have **105**.

Who has the number
that is **ten less** than **125**?

I have **189**.

Who has the number
that is **ten less** than **160**?

I have **115**.

Who has the number
that is **ten less** than **137**?

I have **150**.

Who has the number
that is **ten less** than **129**?

I Have, Who Has?: Math • 1–2 © 2007 Creative Teaching Press

Ten Less — Game B

I have **119**.

Who has the number
that is **ten less** than **117**?

I have **146**.

Who has the number
that is **ten less** than **118**?

I have **107**.

Who has the number
that is **ten less** than **121**?

I have **108**.

Who has the number
that is **ten less** than **113**?

I have **111**.

Who has the number
that is **ten less** than **141**?

I have **103**.

Who has the number
that is **ten less** than **139**?

I have **131**.

Who has the number
that is **ten less** than **156**?

I have **129**.

Who has the number
that is **ten less** than **170**?

I Have, Who Has?: Math • 1–2 © 2007 Creative Teaching Press

Ten Less — Game B

I have **160**.

Who has the number
that is **ten less** than **131**?

I have **200**.

Who has the number
that is **ten less** than **275**?

I have **121**.

Who has the number
that is **ten less** than **114**?

I have **265**.

Who has the number
that is **ten less** than **280**?

I have **104**.

Who has the number
that is **ten less** than **200**?

I have **270**.

Who has the number
that is **ten less** than **215**?

I have **190**.

Who has the number
that is **ten less** than **210**?

I have **205**.

Who has the number
that is **ten less** than **219**?

I have **209**.

Who has the number
that is **ten less** than **222**?

I have **227**.

Who has the number
that is **ten less** than **209**?

I have **212**.

Who has the number
that is **ten less** than **293**?

I have **199**.

Who has the number
that is **ten less** than **211**?

I have **283**.

Who has the number
that is **ten less** than **204**?

I have **201**.

Who has the number
that is **ten less** than **291**?

I have **194**.

Who has the number
that is **ten less** than **237**?

I have **281**.

Who has the **first card**?

I Have, Who Has?: Math • 1–2 © 2007 Creative Teaching Press

Name _____ Date _____

Ten Less — Game B

I Finish the maze by lightly coloring the answers as your classmates say them.

*Start	115	137	144	189	155	218	304	*Finish
101	127	134	143	150	105	281	291	281
105	115	189	107	270	205	283	194	201
107	119	150	111	265	209	212	227	199
111	131	200	255	200	190	104	202	380
106	146	108	103	129	160	121	306	303

II Choose 20 numbers that you did **not** color in the maze above. Write the numbers in the charts below. Rewrite **each** number as **ten less**.

Number from the Maze										
Ten Less										

Number from the Maze										
Ten Less										

Comparing Numbers

I have the **first card**.

Who has the number
that is **greater**: **68** or **15**?

I have **35**.

Who has the number
that is **greater**: **18** or **11**?

I have **68**.

Who has the number
that is **greater**: **27** or **51**?

I have **18**.

Who has the number
that is **greater**: **61** or **49**?

I have **51**.

Who has the number
that is **smaller**: **26** or **72**?

I have **61**.

Who has the number
that is **smaller**: **12** or **30**?

I have **26**.

Who has the number
that is **smaller**: **35** or **80**?

I have **12**.

Who has the number
that is **smaller**: **93** or **79**?

I Have, Who Has?: Math • 1–2 © 2007 Creative Teaching Press

Comparing Numbers

I have **79**.

Who has the number
that is **greater**: **50** or **70**?

I have **9**.

Who has the number
that is **greater**: **83** or **93**?

I have **70**.

Who has the number
that is **greater**: **39** or **53**?

I have **93**.

Who has the number
that is **greater**: **74** or **54**?

I have **53**.

Who has the number
that is **smaller**: **67** or **88**?

I have **74**.

Who has the number
that is **smaller**: **17** or **19**?

I have **67**.

Who has the number
that is **smaller**: **9** or **11**?

I have **17**.

Who has the number
that is **smaller**: **49** or **66**?

Comparing Numbers

I have **49**.

Who has the number that is **greater**: **44** or **39**?

I have **15**.

Who has the number that is **greater**: **11** or **9**?

I have **44**.

Who has the number that is **greater**: **30** or **20**?

I have **11**.

Who has the number that is **greater**: **39** or **50**?

I have **30**.

Who has the number that is **smaller**: **32** or **27**?

I have **50**.

Who has the number that is **smaller**: **72** or **81**?

I have **27**.

Who has the number that is **smaller**: **15** or **19**?

I have **72**.

Who has the number that is **smaller**: **80** or **91**?

I Have, Who Has?: Math • 1–2 © 2007 Creative Teaching Press

Comparing Numbers

I have **80**.

Who has the number
that is **greater**: **38** or **83**?

I have **38**.

Who has the number
that is **greater**: **20** or **39**?

I have **83**.

Who has the number
that is **greater**: **54** or **45**?

I have **39**.

Who has the number
that is **greater**: **56** or **65**?

I have **54**.

Who has the number
that is **smaller**: **32** or **23**?

I have **65**.

Who has the number
that is **smaller**: **42** or **24**?

I have **23**.

Who has the number
that is **smaller**: **83** or **38**?

I have **24**.

Who has the **first card**?

Name _____ Date _____

Comparing Numbers

I Lightly color each number that matches your classmates' answers.

1	2	3	4	5	6	7	8	9	10
11	12	13	14	15	16	17	18	19	20
21	22	23	24	25	26	27	28	29	30
31	32	33	34	35	36	37	38	39	40
41	42	43	44	45	46	47	48	49	50
51	52	53	54	55	56	57	58	59	60
61	62	63	64	65	66	67	68	69	70
71	72	73	74	75	76	77	78	79	80
81	82	83	84	85	86	87	88	89	90
91	92	93	94	95	96	97	98	99	100

II Read each pair of clues to find the mystery number.

1. I am greater than 67 but less than 69. What number am I? _____

2. I am greater than 22 but less than 24. What number am I? _____

3. I am less than 95 but greater than 93. What number am I? _____

I Have, Who Has?: Math • 1–2 © 2007 Creative Teaching Press

Doubles and Doubles + 1

I have the **first card**.

Who has the **double of 5**?

I have **6**.

Who has the **double of 2**?

I have **10**.

Who has the **double of 1**?

I have **4**.

Who has the **double of 7**?

I have **2**.

Who has the **double of 4**?

I have **14**.

Who has the **double of 10**?

I have **8**.

Who has the **double of 3**?

I have **20**.

Who has the **double of 6**?

I Have, Who Has?: Math • 1–2 © 2007 Creative Teaching Press

Doubles and Doubles + 1

I have **12**.

Who has the **double of 9**?

I have **50**.

Who has the **double of 50**?

I have **18**.

Who has the **double of 8**?

I have **100**.

Who has the **double of 30**?

I have **16**.

Who has the **double of 20**?

I have **60**.

Who has the
double of 5 plus 1?

I have **40**.

Who has the **double of 25**?

I have **11**.

Who has the
double of 2 plus 1?

I Have, Who Has?: Math • 1–2 © 2007 Creative Teaching Press

Doubles and Doubles + 1

I have **5**.

Who has the
double of 10 plus 1?

I have **3**.

Who has the
double of 7 plus 1?

I have **21**.

Who has the
double of 4 plus 1?

I have **15**.

Who has the
double of 9 plus 1?

I have **9**.

Who has the
double of 3 plus 1?

I have **19**.

Who has the
double of 6 plus 1?

I have **7**.

Who has the
double of 1 plus 1?

I have **13**.

Who has the
double of 8 plus 1?

I Have, Who Has?, Math • 1–2 © 2007 Creative Teaching Press

Doubles and Doubles + 1

I have **17**.

Who has the **doubles** that equal **0**?

I have **10 + 10**.

Who has the **doubles** that equal **4**?

I have **0 + 0**.

Who has the **doubles** that equal **22**?

I have **2 + 2**.

Who has the **doubles** that equal **8**?

I have **11 + 11**.

Who has the **doubles** that equal **10**?

I have **4 + 4**.

Who has the **doubles** that equal **2**?

I have **5 + 5**.

Who has the **doubles** that equal **20**?

I have **1 + 1**.

Who has the **first card**?

I Have, Who Has?: Math • 1–2 © 2007 Creative Teaching Press

Doubles and Doubles + 1

I Write each number or pair of doubles from left to right as your classmates say the answers.

*Start →							

II Choose 10 numbers from the chart above. Write **the number, the value of double of the number, and the value of that double + 1**. The first one has been done for you.

Number	Double of the Number	Doubles + 1
10	10 + 10 = 20	10 + 10 + 1 = 21

Addition — Game A

I have the **first card**.

Who has the
sum of 2 + 2?

I have **20.**

Who has the
sum of 8 + 2?

I have **4.**

Who has the
sum of 3 + 4?

I have **10.**

Who has the
sum of 6 + 2?

I have **7.**

Who has the
sum of 10 + 1?

I have **8.**

Who has the
sum of 10 + 7?

I have **11.**

Who has the
sum of 10 + 10?

I have **17.**

Who has the
sum of 5 + 4?

I Have, Who Has?: Math • 1–2 © 2007 Creative Teaching Press

Addition — Game A

I have **9**.

Who has the
sum of 0 + 1?

I have **13**.

Who has the
sum of 1 + 1?

I have **1**.

Who has the
sum of 5 + 7?

I have **2**.

Who has the
sum of 9 + 7?

I have **12**.

Who has the
sum of 2 + 1?

I have **16**.

Who has the
sum of 5 + 1?

I have **3**.

Who has the
sum of 10 + 3?

I have **6**.

Who has the
sum of 3 + 2?

Addition — Game A

I have **5**.

Who has the
sum of 12 + 2?

I have **15**.

Who has the
sum of 20 + 10?

I have **14**.

Who has the
sum of 10 + 9?

I have **30**.

Who has the
sum of 20 + 7?

I have **19**.

Who has the
sum of 9 + 9?

I have **27**.

Who has the
sum of 20 + 9?

I have **18**.

Who has the
sum of 14 + 1?

I have **29**.

Who has the
sum of 30 + 2?

I Have, Who Has?: Math • 1–2 © 2007 Creative Teaching Press

Addition — Game A

I have **32**.

Who has the
sum of 30 + 10?

I have **44**.

Who has the
sum of 30 + 9?

I have **40**.

Who has the
sum of 22 + 2?

I have **39**.

Who has the
sum of 10 + 11?

I have **24**.

Who has the
sum of 30 + 1?

I have **21**.

Who has the
sum of 11 + 11?

I have **31**.

Who has the
sum of 42 + 2?

I have **22**.

Who has the **first card?**

I Have, Who Has?: Math • 1-2 © 2007 Creative Teaching Press

Addition — Game A

I Lightly color each number that matches your classmates' answers.

1	2	3	4	5	6	7	8	9	10
11	12	13	14	15	16	17	18	19	20
21	22	23	24	25	26	27	28	29	30
31	32	33	34	35	36	37	38	39	40
41	42	43	44	45	46	47	48	49	50

II Choose 9 numbers from the chart that you did **not** color. Write an **addition number sentence for each number**. The first one has been done for you.

20 + **23** = **43**

_____ + _____ = _____

_____ + _____ = _____

_____ + _____ = _____

_____ + _____ = _____

_____ + _____ = _____

_____ + _____ = _____

_____ + _____ = _____

_____ + _____ = _____

I Have, Who Has?: Math • 1–2 © 2007 Creative Teaching Press

Addition — Game B

I have the **first card**.

Who has the **sum of**
1 + 1 + 1?

I have **23**.

Who has the **sum of**
8 + 8 + 4?

I have **3**.

Who has the **sum of**
5 + 5 + 5?

I have **20**.

Who has the **sum of**
6 + 6 + 1?

I have **15**.

Who has the **sum of**
10 + 10 + 10?

I have **13**.

Who has the **sum of**
5 + 5 + 4?

I have **30**.

Who has the **sum of**
10 + 10 + 3?

I have **14**.

Who has the **sum of**
2 + 2 + 1?

Addition — Game B

I have **5**.

Who has the **sum of**
10 + 10 + 9?

I have **17**.

Who has the **sum of**
20 + 20 + 4?

I have **29**.

Who has the **sum of**
5 + 5 + 1?

I have **44**.

Who has the **sum of**
30 + 30 + 3?

I have **11**.

Who has the **sum of**
0 + 0 + 1?

I have **63**.

Who has the **sum of**
20 + 20 + 10?

I have **1**.

Who has the **sum of**
8 + 8 + 1?

I have **50**.

Who has the **sum of**
30 + 30 + 9?

I Have, Who Has?: Math • 1–2 © 2007 Creative Teaching Press

Addition — Game B

I have **69**.

Who has the **sum of**
2 + 2 + 2?

I have **16**.

Who has the **sum of**
8 + 8 + 2?

I have **6**.

Who has the **sum of**
2 + 2 + 0?

I have **18**.

Who has the **sum of**
20 + 10 + 10?

I have **4**.

Who has the **sum of**
0 + 6 + 6?

I have **40**.

Who has the **sum of**
25 + 25 + 10?

I have **12**.

Who has the **sum of**
5 + 5 + 6?

I have **60**.

Who has the **sum of**
25 + 25 + 1?

Addition — Game B

I have **51**.

Who has the **sum of**
20 + 20 + 3?

I have **7**.

Who has the **sum of**
15 + 5 + 5?

I have **43**.

Who has the **sum of**
40 + 40 + 5?

I have **25**.

Who has the **sum of**
20 + 10 + 5?

I have **85**.

Who has the **sum of**
10 + 10 + 11?

I have **35**.

Who has the **sum of**
20 + 10 + 7?

I have **31**.

Who has the **sum of**
2 + 2 + 3?

I have **37**.

Who has the **first card**?

I Have, Who Has?: Math • 1–2 © 2007 Creative Teaching Press

Name _____ Date _____

Addition — Game B

I Write each number from left to right as your classmates say the answers.

*Start →							

II Choose 10 numbers from the chart above. Write **an addition number sentence using three terms for each number**. The first one has been done for you.

_____2_____ + _____15_____ + _____13_____ = _____30_____

_____ + _____ + _____ = _____

_____ + _____ + _____ = _____

_____ + _____ + _____ = _____

_____ + _____ + _____ = _____

_____ + _____ + _____ = _____

_____ + _____ + _____ = _____

_____ + _____ + _____ = _____

_____ + _____ + _____ = _____

_____ + _____ + _____ = _____

_____ + _____ + _____ = _____

Commutative Property of Addition

I have the **first card**.

Who has the **set of numbers** that means the same thing as **5 + 7**?

I have **6 + 8**.

Who has the **set of numbers** that means the same thing as **3 + 8**?

I have **7 + 5**.

Who has the **set of numbers** that means the same thing as **1 + 9**?

I have **8 + 3**.

Who has the **set of numbers** that means the same thing as **1 + 4**?

I have **9 + 1**.

Who has the **set of numbers** that means the same thing as **4 + 2**?

I have **4 + 1**.

Who has the **set of numbers** that means the same thing as **8 + 9**?

I have **2 + 4**.

Who has the **set of numbers** that means the same thing as **8 + 6**?

I have **9 + 8**.

Who has the **set of numbers** that means the same thing as **4 + 3**?

I Have, Who Has?: Math • 1–2 © 2007 Creative Teaching Press

Commutative Property of Addition

I have **3 + 4**.

Who has the **set of numbers** that means the same thing as **1 + 2**?

I have **9 + 5**.

Who has the **set of numbers** that means the same thing as **7 + 1**?

I have **2 + 1**.

Who has the **set of numbers** that means the same thing as **8 + 1**?

I have **1 + 7**.

Who has the **set of numbers** that means the same thing as **8 + 2**?

I have **1 + 8**.

Who has the **set of numbers** that means the same thing as **6 + 4**?

I have **2 + 8**.

Who has the **set of numbers** that means the same thing as **7 + 9**?

I have **4 + 6**.

Who has the **set of numbers** that means the same thing as **5 + 9**?

I have **9 + 7**.

Who has the **set of numbers** that means the same thing as **2 + 6**?

I have **6 + 2**.

Who has the **set of numbers** that means the same thing as **9 + 3**?

I have **5 + 1**.

Who has the **set of numbers** that means the same thing as **7 + 2**?

I have **3 + 9**.

Who has the **set of numbers** that means the same thing as **5 + 6**?

I have **2 + 7**.

Who has the **set of numbers** that means the same thing as **5 + 3**?

I have **6 + 5**.

Who has the **set of numbers** that means the same thing as **7 + 4**?

I have **3 + 5**.

Who has the **set of numbers** that means the same thing as **4 + 9**?

I have **4 + 7**.

Who has the **set of numbers** that means the same thing as **1 + 5**?

I have **9 + 4**.

Who has the **set of numbers** that means the same thing as **1 + 6**?

Commutative Property of Addition

I have **6 + 1**.

Who has the **set of numbers** that means the same thing as **7 + 3**?

I have **3 + 2**.

Who has the **set of numbers** that means the same thing as **8 + 5**?

I have **3 + 7**.

Who has the **set of numbers** that means the same thing as **8 + 4**?

I have **5 + 8**.

Who has the **set of numbers** that means the same thing as **6 + 7**?

I have **4 + 8**.

Who has the **set of numbers** that means the same thing as **6 + 9**?

I have **7 + 6**.

Who has the **set of numbers** that means the same thing as **3 + 1**?

I have **9 + 6**.

Who has the **set of numbers** that means the same thing as **2 + 3**?

I have **1 + 3**.

Who has the **first card**?

I Have, Who Has? Math • 1–2 © 2007 Creative Teaching Press

Commutative Property of Addition

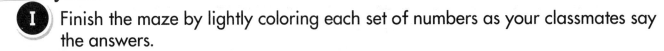

I Finish the maze by lightly coloring each set of numbers as your classmates say the answers.

*Start	7 + 5	3 + 2	2 + 1	1 + 8	4 + 6	3 + 4	1 + 9
2 + 4	9 + 1	9 + 8	3 + 4	5 + 7	9 + 5	1 + 7	2 + 8
6 + 8	8 + 3	4 + 1	2 + 5	5 + 1	4 + 7	5 + 7	9 + 7
5 + 8	6 + 7	9 + 4	3 + 5	2 + 7	6 + 5	3 + 9	6 + 2
2 + 9	3 + 7	6 + 1	4 + 6	2 + 9	1 + 4	5 + 4	3 + 6
5 + 1	4 + 8	9 + 6	3 + 2	5 + 8	7 + 6	1 + 3	*Finish

II Choose 10 sets of numbers that you did **not** color. Write **the set of numbers on the left and the commutative property for the set of numbers on the right.**

Example: 5 + 7 = 7 + 5

_____ + _____ = _____ + _____   _____ + _____ = _____ + _____

_____ + _____ = _____ + _____   _____ + _____ = _____ + _____

_____ + _____ = _____ + _____   _____ + _____ = _____ + _____

_____ + _____ = _____ + _____   _____ + _____ = _____ + _____

_____ + _____ = _____ + _____   _____ + _____ = _____ + _____

I Have, Who Has?: Math • 1–2 © 2007 Creative Teaching Press

Subtraction — Game A

I have the **first card**.

Who has the
difference of 5 − 1?

I have **1**.

Who has the
difference of 13 − 0?

I have **4**.

Who has the
difference of 9 − 1?

I have **13**.

Who has the
difference of 14 − 2?

I have **8**.

Who has the
difference of 7 − 2?

I have **12**.

Who has the
difference of 20 − 10?

I have **5**.

Who has the
difference of 9 − 8?

I have **10**.

Who has the
difference of 16 − 2?

Subtraction — Game A

I have **14**.

Who has the
difference of 5 – 2?

I have **15**.

Who has the
difference of 25 – 5?

I have **3**.

Who has the
difference of 8 – 6?

I have **20**.

Who has the
difference of 20 – 1?

I have **2**.

Who has the
difference of 10 – 4?

I have **19**.

Who has the
difference of 10 – 3?

I have **6**.

Who has the
difference of 20 – 5?

I have **7**.

Who has the
difference of 15 – 4?

I Have, Who Has?: Math • 1–2 © 2007 Creative Teaching Press

Subtraction — Game A

I have **11**.

Who has the
difference of 26 – 10?

I have **18**.

Who has the
difference of 30 – 1?

I have **16**.

Who has the
difference of 27 – 2?

I have **29**.

Who has the
difference of 20 – 3?

I have **25**.

Who has the
difference of 19 – 10?

I have **17**.

Who has the
difference of 27 – 0?

I have **9**.

Who has the
difference of 20 – 2?

I have **27**.

Who has the
difference of 30 – 4?

Subtraction — Game A

I have **26**.

Who has the
difference of 40 – 10?

I have **31**.

Who has the
difference of 35 – 3?

I have **30**.

Who has the
difference of 45 – 2?

I have **32**.

Who has the
difference of 47 – 2?

I have **43**.

Who has the
difference of 41 – 2?

I have **45**.

Who has the
difference of 40 – 5?

I have **39**.

Who has the
difference of 41 – 10?

I have **35**.

Who has the **first card?**

I Have, Who Has?: Math • 1–2 © 2007 Creative Teaching Press

Subtraction — Game A

I Lightly color each number that matches your classmates' answers.

1	2	3	4	5	6	7	8	9	10
11	12	13	14	15	16	17	18	19	20
21	22	23	24	25	26	27	28	29	30
31	32	33	34	35	36	37	38	39	40
41	42	43	44	45	46	47	48	49	50

II Choose 9 numbers from the chart that you did **not** color. Write a **subtraction number sentence for each number**. The first one has been done for you.

_____34_____ – _____10_____ = _____24_____

_____ – _____ = _____

_____ – _____ = _____

_____ – _____ = _____

_____ – _____ = _____

_____ – _____ = _____

_____ – _____ = _____

_____ – _____ = _____

_____ – _____ = _____

Subtraction — Game B

I have the **first card**.

Who has the **difference of 5 – 4**?

I have **20**.

Who has the **difference of 15 – 5**?

I have **1**.

Who has the **difference of 11 – 6**?

I have **10**.

Who has the **difference of 20 – 3**?

I have **5**.

Who has the **difference of 20 – 2**?

I have **17**.

Who has the **difference of 40 – 10**?

I have **18**.

Who has the **difference of 40 – 20**?

I have **30**.

Who has the **difference of 10 – 7**?

I Have, Who Has?: Math • 1–2 © 2007 Creative Teaching Press

Subtraction — Game B

I have **3**.

Who has the **difference of 20 − 6**?

I have **29**.

Who has the **difference of 10 − 8**?

I have **14**.

Who has the **difference of 30 − 7**?

I have **2**.

Who has the **difference of 80 − 6**?

I have **23**.

Who has the **difference of 50 − 6**?

I have **74**.

Who has the **difference of 56 − 6**?

I have **44**.

Who has the **difference of 35 − 6**?

I have **50**.

Who has the **difference of 49 − 10**?

Subtraction — Game B

I have **39**.

Who has the **difference of 40 – 6?**

I have **38**.

Who has the **difference of 60 – 20?**

I have **34**.

Who has the **difference of 15 – 6?**

I have **40**.

Who has the **difference of 69 – 9?**

I have **9**.

Who has the **difference of 20 – 7?**

I have **60**.

Who has the **difference of 70 – 7?**

I have **13**.

Who has the **difference of 45 – 7?**

I have **63**.

Who has the **difference of 55 – 4?**

I Have, Who Has?: Math • 1–2 © 2007 Creative Teaching Press

Subtraction — Game B

I have **51**.

Who has the **difference of 90 – 6**?

I have **81**.

Who has the **difference of 42 – 11**?

I have **84**.

Who has the **difference of 85 – 6**?

I have **31**.

Who has the **difference of 80 – 11**?

I have **79**.

Who has the **difference of 65 – 6**?

I have **69**.

Who has the **difference of 90 – 12**?

I have **59**.

Who has the **difference of 92 – 11**?

I have **78**.

Who has the **first card**?

Name _____ Date _____

Subtraction — Game B

I Write each number from left to right as your classmates say the answers.

*Start →						

II Choose 10 numbers from the chart above. Write **a subtraction number sentence for each number**. The first one has been done for you.

$$\underline{\quad 30 \quad} - \underline{\quad 6 \quad} = \underline{\quad 24 \quad}$$

$$\underline{\qquad} - \underline{\qquad} = \underline{\qquad}$$

$$\underline{\qquad} - \underline{\qquad} = \underline{\qquad}$$

$$\underline{\qquad} - \underline{\qquad} = \underline{\qquad}$$

$$\underline{\qquad} - \underline{\qquad} = \underline{\qquad}$$

$$\underline{\qquad} - \underline{\qquad} = \underline{\qquad}$$

$$\underline{\qquad} - \underline{\qquad} = \underline{\qquad}$$

$$\underline{\qquad} - \underline{\qquad} = \underline{\qquad}$$

$$\underline{\qquad} - \underline{\qquad} = \underline{\qquad}$$

$$\underline{\qquad} - \underline{\qquad} = \underline{\qquad}$$

I Have, Who Has?: Math • 1–2 © 2007 Creative Teaching Press

Fact Families — Game A

I have the **first card.**

Who has the missing
**subtraction facts for
1 + 2 = 3 and 2 + 1 = 3?**

I have **4 – 1 = 3**
and 4 – 3 = 1.

Who has the missing
**subtraction facts for
7 + 2 = 9 and 2 + 7 = 9?**

I have **3 – 1 = 2**
and 3 – 2 = 1.

Who has the missing
**subtraction facts for
2 + 4 = 6 and 4 + 2 = 6?**

I have **9 – 2 = 7**
and 9 – 7 = 2.

Who has the missing
**subtraction facts for
3 + 8 = 11 and 8 + 3 = 11?**

I have **6 – 2 = 4**
and 6 – 4 = 2.

Who has the missing
**subtraction facts for
3 + 5 = 8 and 5 + 3 = 8?**

I have **11 – 3 = 8**
and 11 – 8 = 3.

Who has the missing
**subtraction facts for
1 + 7 = 8 and 7 + 1 = 8?**

I have **8 – 3 = 5**
and 8 – 5 = 3.

Who has the missing
**subtraction facts for
1 + 3 = 4 and 3 + 1 = 4?**

I have **8 – 1 = 7**
and 8 – 7 = 1.

Who has the missing
**subtraction facts for
9 + 2 = 11 and 2 + 9 = 11?**

Fact Families — Game A

I have **11 − 2 = 9**
and **11 − 9 = 2**.

Who has the missing
**subtraction facts for
3 + 4 = 7 and 4 + 3 = 7?**

I have **5 − 1 = 4**
and **5 − 4 = 1**.

Who has the missing
**subtraction facts for
2 + 3 = 5 and 3 + 2 = 5?**

I have **7 − 3 = 4**
and **7 − 4 = 3**.

Who has the missing
**subtraction facts for
1 + 6 = 7 and 6 + 1 = 7?**

I have **5 − 2 = 3**
and **5 − 3 = 2**.

Who has the missing
**subtraction facts for
8 + 1 = 9 and 1 + 8 = 9?**

I have **7 − 1 = 6**
and **7 − 6 = 1**.

Who has the missing
**subtraction facts for
3 + 6 = 9 and 6 + 3 = 9?**

I have **9 − 1 = 8**
and **9 − 8 = 1**.

Who has the missing
**subtraction facts for
3 + 7 = 10 and 7 + 3 = 10?**

I have **9 − 3 = 6**
and **9 − 6 = 3**.

Who has the missing
**subtraction facts for
4 + 1 = 5 and 1 + 4 = 5?**

I have **10 − 3 = 7**
and **10 − 7 = 3**.

Who has the missing
**subtraction facts for
2 + 5 = 7 and 5 + 2 = 7?**

I Have, Who Has?: Math • 1–2 © 2007 Creative Teaching Press

Fact Families — Game A

I have **7 – 2 = 5**
and **7 – 5 = 2**.

Who has the missing
subtraction facts for
9 + 3 = 12 and 3 + 9 = 12?

I have **9 – 4 = 5**
and **9 – 5 = 4**.

Who has the missing
subtraction facts for
5 + 6 = 11 and 6 + 5 = 11?

I have **12 – 3 = 9**
and **12 – 9 = 3**.

Who has the missing
subtraction facts for
1 + 5 = 6 and 5 + 1 = 6?

I have **11 – 5 = 6**
and **11 – 6 = 5**.

Who has the missing
subtraction facts for
3 + 10 = 13 and 10 + 3 = 13?

I have **6 – 5 = 1**
and **6 – 1 = 5**.

Who has the missing
subtraction facts for
10 + 2 = 12 and 2 + 10 = 12?

I have **13 – 3 = 10**
and **13 – 10 = 3**.

Who has the missing
subtraction facts for
5 + 10 = 15 and 10 + 5 = 15?

I have **12 – 2 = 10**
and **12 – 10 = 2**.

Who has the missing
subtraction facts for
4 + 5 = 9 and 5 + 4 = 9?

I have **15 – 5 = 10**
and **15 – 10 = 5**.

Who has the missing
subtraction facts for
4 + 6 = 10 and 6 + 4 = 10?

Fact Families — Game A

I have **10 – 4 = 6**
and 10 – 6 = 4.

Who has the missing
subtraction facts for
5 + 8 = 13 and 8 + 5 = 13?

I have **13 – 6 = 7**
and 13 – 7 = 6.

Who has the missing
subtraction facts for
8 + 4 = 12 and 4 + 8 = 12?

I have **13 – 5 = 8**
and 13 – 8 = 5.

Who has the missing
subtraction facts for
4 + 7 = 11 and 7 + 4 = 11?

I have **12 – 4 = 8**
and 12 – 8 = 4.

Who has the missing
subtraction facts for
4 + 9 = 13 and 9 + 4 = 13?

I have **11 – 4 = 7**
and 11 – 7 = 4.

Who has the missing
subtraction facts for
5 + 9 = 14 and 9 + 5 = 14?

I have **13 – 4 = 9**
and 13 – 9 = 4.

Who has the missing
subtraction facts for
6 + 8 = 14 and 8 + 6 = 14?

I have **14 – 5 = 9**
and 14 – 9 = 5.

Who has the missing
subtraction facts for
6 + 7 = 13 and 7 + 6 = 13?

I have **14 – 6 = 8**
and 14 – 8 = 6.

Who has the **first card**?

I Have, Who Has?: Math • 1–2 © 2007 Creative Teaching Press

Name _____ Date _____

Fact Families — Game A

I Finish the maze by lightly coloring the subtraction facts as your classmates say them.

*Start	8 – 3 = 5 8 – 5 = 3	4 – 1 = 3 4 – 3 = 1	7 – 3 = 4 7 – 4 = 3	7 – 1 = 6 7 – 6 = 1	9 – 3 = 6 9 – 6 = 3
3 – 1 = 2 3 – 2 = 1	6 – 2 = 4 6 – 4 = 2	9 – 2 = 7 9 – 7 = 2	11 – 2 = 9 11 – 9 = 2	7 – 2 = 5 7 – 5 = 2	5 – 1 = 4 5 – 4 = 1
13 – 3 = 10 13 – 10 = 3	11 – 5 = 6 11 – 6 = 5	11 – 3 = 8 11 – 8 = 3	8 – 1 = 7 8 – 7 = 1	9 – 1 = 8 9 – 8 = 1	5 – 2 = 3 5 – 3 = 2
15 – 5 = 10 15 – 10 = 5	9 – 4 = 5 9 – 5 = 4	12 – 2 = 10 12 – 10 = 2	6 – 5 = 1 6 – 1 = 5	10 – 3 = 7 10 – 7 = 3	9 – 3 = 6 9 – 6 = 3
10 – 4 = 6 10 – 6 = 4	12 – 5 = 7 12 – 7 = 5	9 – 3 = 6 9 – 6 = 3	12 – 3 = 9 12 – 9 = 3	7 – 2 = 5 7 – 5 = 2	10 – 1 = 9 10 – 9 = 1
13 – 5 = 8 13 – 8 = 5	11 – 4 = 7 11 – 7 = 4	14 – 5 = 9 14 – 9 = 5	10 – 2 = 8 10 – 8 = 2	15 – 6 = 9 15 – 9 = 6	*Finish
13 – 6 = 7 13 – 7 = 6	12 – 4 = 8 12 – 8 = 4	13 – 6 = 7 13 – 7 = 6	12 – 4 = 8 12 – 8 = 4	13 – 4 = 9 13 – 9 = 4	14 – 6 = 8 14 – 8 = 6

II Choose 4 subtraction facts that you **did not** color. Write the subtraction facts below. Then write the **addition facts** that are missing to complete the fact family. An example has been done for you.

5 – 2 = 3				
5 – 3 = 2				
2 + 3 = 5				
3 + 2 = 5				

Fact Families — Game B

I have the **first card**.

Who has the missing
addition facts for
3 – 1 = 2 and 3 – 2 = 1?

I have **1 + 5 = 6**
and 5 + 1 = 6.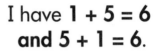

Who has the missing
addition facts for
9 – 2 = 7 and 9 – 7 = 2?

I have **1 + 2 = 3**
and 2 + 1 = 3.

Who has the missing
addition facts for
6 – 2 = 4 and 6 – 4 = 2?

I have **2 + 7 = 9**
and 7 + 2 = 9.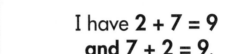

Who has the missing
addition facts for
11 – 8 = 3 and 11 – 3 = 8?

I have **2 + 4 = 6**
and 4 + 2 = 6.

Who has the missing
addition facts for
8 – 5 = 3 and 8 – 3 = 5?

I have **3 + 8 = 11**
and 8 + 3 = 11.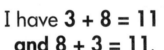

Who has the missing
addition facts for
8 – 1 = 7 and 8 – 7 = 1?

I have **3 + 5 = 8**
and 5 + 3 = 8.

Who has the missing
addition facts for
6 – 1 = 5 and 6 – 5 = 1?

I have **1 + 7 = 8**
and 7 + 1 = 8.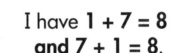

Who has the missing
addition facts for
12 – 9 = 3 and 12 – 3 = 9?

I Have, Who Has?: Math • *1–2* © 2007 Creative Teaching Press

Fact Families — Game B

I have **3 + 9 = 12**
and **9 + 3 = 12**.

Who has the missing
addition facts for
4 − 1 = 3 and 4 − 3 = 1?

I have **2 + 6 = 8**
and **6 + 2 = 8**.

Who has the missing
addition facts for
10 − 7 = 3 and 10 − 3 = 7?

I have **1 + 3 = 4**
and **3 + 1 = 4**.

Who has the missing
addition facts for
7 − 2 = 5 and 7 − 5 = 2?

I have **3 + 7 = 10**
and **7 + 3 = 10**.

Who has the missing
addition facts for
7 − 1 = 6 and 7 − 6 = 1?

I have **2 + 5 = 7**
and **5 + 2 = 7**.

Who has the missing
addition facts for
5 − 1 = 4 and 5 − 4 = 1?

I have **1 + 6 = 7**
and **6 + 1 = 7**.

Who has the missing
addition facts for
11 − 2 = 9 and 11 − 9 = 2?

I have **1 + 4 = 5**
and **4 + 1 = 5**.

Who has the missing
addition facts for
8 − 2 = 6 and 8 − 6 = 2?

I have **2 + 9 = 11**
and **9 + 2 = 11**.

Who has the missing
addition facts for
7 − 4 = 3 and 7 − 3 = 4?

Fact Families — Game B

I have **3 + 4 = 7**
and 4 + 3 = 7.

Who has the missing
addition facts for
9 − 1 = 8 and 9 − 8 = 1?

I have **3 + 10 = 13**
and 10 + 3 = 13.

Who has the missing
addition facts for
10 − 2 = 8 and 10 − 8 = 2?

I have **1 + 8 = 9**
and 8 + 1 = 9.

Who has the missing
addition facts for
12 − 2 = 10 and 12 − 10 = 2?

I have **2 + 8 = 10**
and 8 + 2 = 10.

Who has the missing
addition facts for
9 − 6 = 3 and 9 − 3 = 6?

I have **2 + 10 = 12**
and 10 + 2 = 12.

Who has the missing
addition facts for
10 − 1 = 9 and 10 − 9 = 1?

I have **3 + 6 = 9**
and 6 + 3 = 9.

Who has the missing
addition facts for
16 − 6 = 10 and 16 − 10 = 6?

I have **1 + 9 = 10**
and 9 + 1 = 10.

Who has the missing
addition facts for
13 − 10 = 3 and 13 − 3 = 10?

I have **6 + 10 = 16**
and 10 + 6 = 16.

Who has the missing
addition facts for
12 − 4 = 8 and 12 − 8 = 4?

Fact Families – Game B

I have 4 + 8 = 12
and 8 + 4 = 12.

Who has the missing
addition facts for
11 – 5 = 6 and 11 – 6 = 5?

I have 6 + 7 = 13
and 7 + 6 = 13.

Who has the missing
addition facts for
9 – 4 = 5 and 9 – 5 = 4?

I have 5 + 6 = 11
and 6 + 5 = 11.

Who has the missing
addition facts for
15 – 7 = 8 and 15 – 8 = 7?

I have 4 + 5 = 9
and 5 + 4 = 9.

Who has the missing
addition facts for
13 – 5 = 8 and 13 – 8 = 5?

I have 7 + 8 = 15
and 8 + 7 = 15.

Who has the missing
addition facts for
5 – 2 = 3 and 5 – 3 = 2?

I have 5 + 8 = 13
and 8 + 5 = 13.

Who has the missing
addition facts for
10 – 4 = 6 and 10 – 6 = 4?

I have 2 + 3 = 5
and 3 + 2 = 5.

Who has the missing
addition facts for
13 – 6 = 7 and 13 – 7 = 6?

I have 4 + 6 = 10
and 6 + 4 = 10.

Who has the **first card**?

Name _____ Date _____

Fact Families Card Game B

I Finish the maze by lightly coloring the addition facts as your classmates say them.

*Start	$1 + 2 = 3$ $2 + 1 = 3$	$2 + 4 = 6$ $4 + 2 = 6$	$3 + 5 = 8$ $5 + 3 = 8$	$1 + 5 = 6$ $5 + 1 = 6$	$2 + 7 = 9$ $7 + 2 = 9$
$4 + 6 = 10$ $6 + 4 = 10$	$5 + 4 = 9$ $4 + 5 = 9$	$1 + 4 = 5$ $4 + 1 = 5$	$2 + 5 = 7$ $5 + 2 = 7$	$1 + 3 = 4$ $3 + 1 = 4$	$3 + 8 = 11$ $8 + 3 = 11$
$1 + 6 = 7$ $6 + 1 = 7$	$3 + 7 = 10$ $7 + 3 = 10$	$2 + 6 = 8$ $6 + 2 = 8$	$7 + 2 = 9$ $2 + 7 = 9$	$3 + 9 = 12$ $9 + 3 = 12$	$1 + 7 = 8$ $7 + 1 = 8$
$2 + 9 = 11$ $9 + 2 = 11$	$7 + 5 = 12$ $5 + 7 = 12$	$4 + 5 = 9$ $5 + 4 = 9$	$5 + 8 = 13$ $8 + 5 = 13$	$6 + 9 = 15$ $9 + 6 = 15$	$4 + 7 = 11$ $7 + 4 = 11$
$3 + 4 = 7$ $4 + 3 = 7$	$1 + 8 = 9$ $8 + 1 = 9$	$6 + 7 = 13$ $7 + 6 = 13$	$5 + 6 = 11$ $6 + 5 = 11$	$7 + 8 = 15$ $8 + 7 = 15$	$5 + 10 = 15$ $10 + 5 = 15$
$4 + 9 = 13$ $9 + 4 = 13$	$2 + 10 = 12$ $10 + 2 = 12$	$2 + 3 = 5$ $3 + 2 = 5$	$4 + 8 = 12$ $8 + 4 = 12$	$2 + 3 = 5$ $3 + 2 = 5$	$6 + 7 = 13$ $7 + 6 = 13$
$4 + 10 = 14$ $10 + 4 = 14$	$1 + 9 = 10$ $9 + 1 = 10$	$3 + 10 = 13$ $10 + 3 = 13$	$6 + 10 = 16$ $10 + 6 = 16$	$5 + 8 = 13$ $8 + 5 = 13$	$4 + 5 = 9$ $5 + 4 = 9$
$3 + 8 = 11$ $8 + 3 = 11$	$3 + 5 = 8$ $5 + 3 = 8$	$2 + 8 = 10$ $8 + 2 = 10$	$3 + 6 = 9$ $6 + 3 = 9$	$4 + 6 = 10$ $6 + 4 = 10$	*Finish

II Choose 4 addition facts that you **did not** color. Write the addition facts below. Then write the **subtraction facts** that are missing to complete the fact family. An example has been done for you.

$4 + 6 = 10$				
$6 + 4 = 10$				
$10 - 4 = 6$				
$10 - 6 = 4$				

I Have, Who Has?: Math • 1–2 © 2007 Creative Teaching Press

Multiplication

I have the **first card**.

Who has **1 group of 7**?

I have **39**.

Who has **1 group of 500**?

I have **7**.

Who has **1 group of 13**?

I have **500**.

Who has **2 groups of 1**?

I have **13**.

Who has **1 group of 26**?

I have **2**.

Who has **2 groups of 5**?

I have **26**.

Who has **1 group of 39**?

I have **10**.

Who has **2 groups of 2**?

Multiplication

I have **4**.

Who has **2 groups of 10**?

I have **60**.

Who has **2 groups of 40**?

I have **20**.

Who has **2 groups of 25**?

I have **80**.

Who has **3 groups of 2**?

I have **50**.

Who has **2 groups of 50**?

I have **6**.

Who has **3 groups of 1**?

I have **100**.

Who has **2 groups of 30**?

I have **3**.

Who has **3 groups of 10**?

I Have, Who Has?: Math • 1–2 © 2007 Creative Teaching Press

Multiplication

I have **30**.

Who has **3 groups of 25**?

I have **25**.

Who has **2 groups of 12**?

I have **75**.

Who has **3 groups of 30**?

I have **24**.

Who has **2 groups of 7**?

I have **90**.

Who has **3 groups of 5**?

I have **14**.

Who has **1 group of 1**?

I have **15**.

Who has **5 groups of 5**?

I have **1**.

Who has **5 groups of 1**?

I Have, Who Has?: Math • 1–2 © 2007 Creative Teaching Press

I have **5**.

Who has **4 groups of 2**?

I have **12**.

Who has **2 groups of 11**?

I have **8**.

Who has **4 groups of 10**?

I have **22**.

Who has **8 groups of 2**?

I have **40**.

Who has **3 groups of 3**?

I have **16**.

Who has **2 groups of 9**?

I have **9**.

Who has **2 groups of 6**?

I have **18**.

Who has the **first card**?

I Have, Who Has?: Math • 1–2 © 2007 Creative Teaching Press

Name _____ Date _____

Multiplication

I Write each number from left to right as your classmates say the answers.

*Start →							
A	**B**	**C**	**D**	**E**	**F**	**G**	**H**

II Read each pair of clues to answer the multiplication problems.

1. It equals 1 group of 100. It is in column D. What is the number? _____

2. It equals 2 groups of 10. It is in column B. What is the number? _____

3. It equals 3 groups of 30. It is in column C. What is the number? _____

4. It equals 1 group of 3. It is in column H. What is the number? _____

5. It equals 4 groups of 2. It is in column B. What is the number? _____

6. It equals 4 groups of 20. It is in column F. What is the number? _____

7. It equals 1 group of 5. It is in column A. What is the number? _____

8. It equals 3 groups of 25. It is in column B. What is the number? _____

9. It equals 5 groups of 5. It is in column E. What is the number? _____

10. It equals 2 groups of 2. It is in column A. What is the number? _____

Patterns — Game A

I have the **first card**.

Who has the number that comes next in this **pattern: 1, 2, 3, ___?**

I have **1**.

Who has the number that comes next in this **pattern: 2, 4, 6, ___?**

I have **4**.

Who has the number that comes next in this **pattern: 10, 9, 8, ___?**

I have **8**.

Who has the number that comes next in this **pattern: 0, 1, 2, ___?**

I have **7**.

Who has the number that comes next in this **pattern: 6, 7, 8, ___?**

I have **3**.

Who has the number that comes next in this **pattern: 8, 6, 4, ___?**

I have **9**.

Who has the number that comes next in this **pattern: 4, 3, 2, ___?**

I have **2**.

Who has the number that comes next in this **pattern: 40, 30, 20, ___?**

I Have, Who Has?: Math • 1–2 © 2007 Creative Teaching Press

Patterns — Game A

I have **10**.

Who has the number
that comes next in this
pattern: 20, 15, 10, ___?

I have **31**.

Who has the number
that comes next in this
pattern: 25, 30, 35, ___?

I have **5**.

Who has the number
that comes next in this
pattern: 5, 10, 15, ___?

I have **40**.

Who has the number
that comes next in this
pattern: 90, 80, 70, ___?

I have **20**.

Who has the number
that comes next in this
pattern: 20, 40, 60, ___?

I have **60**.

Who has the number
that comes next in this
pattern: 25, 50, 75, ___?

I have **80**.

Who has the number
that comes next in this
pattern: 61, 51, 41, ___?

I have **100**.

Who has the number
that comes next in this
pattern: 93, 83, 73, ___?

I Have, Who Has?: Math • 1–2 © 2007 Creative Teaching Press

Patterns — Game A

I have **63**.

Who has the number that comes next in this **pattern: 14, 24, 34, ___?**

I have **25**.

Who has the number that comes next in this **pattern: 89, 79, 69, ___?**

I have **44**.

Who has the number that comes next in this **pattern: 20, 21, 22, ___?**

I have **59**.

Who has the number that comes next in this **pattern: 95, 85, 75, ___?**

I have **23**.

Who has the number that comes next in this **pattern: 16, 15, 14, ___?**

I have **65**.

Who has the number that comes next in this **pattern: 18, 28, 38, ___?**

I have **13**.

Who has the number that comes next in this **pattern: 10, 15, 20, ___?**

I have **48**.

Who has the number that comes next in this **pattern: 66, 56, 46, ___?**

I Have, Who Has?: Math • 1–2 © 2007 Creative Teaching Press

Patterns — Game A

I have **36**.

Who has the number that comes next in this **pattern: 20, 25, 30, ___?**

I have **66**.

Who has the number that comes next in this **pattern: 66, 55, 44, ___?**

I have **35**.

Who has the number that comes next in this **pattern: 5, 7, 9, ___?**

I have **33**.

Who has the number that comes next in this **pattern: 20, 30, 40, ___?**

I have **11**.

Who has the number that comes next in this **pattern: 17, 27, 37, ___?**

I have **50**.

Who has the number that comes next in this **pattern: 42, 32, 22, ___?**

I have **47**.

Who has the number that comes next in this **pattern: 99, 88, 77, ___?**

I have **12**.

Who has the **first card**?

I Have, Who Has?: Math • 1–2 © 2007 Creative Teaching Press

Patterns — Game A

I Lightly color each number that matches your classmates' answers.

1	2	3	4	5	6	7	8	9	10
11	12	13	14	15	16	17	18	19	20
21	22	23	24	25	26	27	28	29	30
31	32	33	34	35	36	37	38	39	40
41	42	43	44	45	46	47	48	49	50
51	52	53	54	55	56	57	58	59	60
61	62	63	64	65	66	67	68	69	70
71	72	73	74	75	76	77	78	79	80
81	82	83	84	85	86	87	88	89	90
91	92	93	94	95	96	97	98	99	100

II Choose 2 numbers from the hundred chart that you did **not** color. Use those numbers to create **2 different patterns**. Then, trade with a partner to extend the patterns created.

My Number Pattern	Extended Pattern Completed by: _____

I Have, Who Has?: Math • 1–2 © 2007 Creative Teaching Press

Patterns — Game B

I have the **first card**.

Who has the missing number in this **pattern**: 2, 4, 6, ___, 10?

I have **6**.

Who has the missing number in this **pattern**: 0, ___, 10, 15, 20?

I have **8**.

Who has the missing number in this **pattern**: 1, 3, 5, ___, 9?

I have **5**.

Who has the missing number in this **pattern**: 4, 14, ___, 34, 44?

I have **7**.

Who has the missing number in this **pattern**: 1, 2, ___, 4, 5?

I have **24**.

Who has the missing number in this **pattern**: 55, 44, 33, ___, 11?

I have **3**.

Who has the missing number in this **pattern**: 9, 8, 7, ___, 5?

I have **22**.

Who has the missing number in this **pattern**: 10, 20, 30, ___, 50?

I have **40**.

Who has the missing number in this **pattern**: 9, 19, 29, ___, 49?

I have **15**.

Who has the missing number in this **pattern**: 91, 81, 71, ___, 51?

I have **39**.

Who has the missing number in this **pattern**: 10, 8, 6, ___, 2?

I have **61**.

Who has the missing number in this **pattern**: 30, 35, 40, ___, 50?

I have **4**.

Who has the missing number in this **pattern**: 30, 40, 50, ___, 70?

I have **45**.

Who has the missing number in this **pattern**: 66, 65, 64, ___, 62?

I have **60**.

Who has the missing number in this **pattern**: 5, 10, ___, 20, 25?

I have **63**.

Who has the missing number in this **pattern**: 54, 64, 74, ___, 94?

Patterns — Game B

I have **84**.

Who has the missing number in this **pattern**: 8, 6, 4, ___, 0?

I have **11**.

Who has the missing number in this **pattern**: 13, 23, 33, ___, 53?

I have **2**.

Who has the missing number in this **pattern**: 20, 30, 40, ___, 60?

I have **43**.

Who has the missing number in this **pattern**: 68, 58, 48, ___, 28?

I have the **50**.

Who has the missing number in this **pattern**: 85, 80, 75, ___, 65?

I have **38**.

Who has the missing number in this **pattern**: 35, 30, 25, ___, 15?

I have **70**.

Who has the missing number in this **pattern**: 41, 31, 21, ___, 1?

I have **20**.

Who has the missing number in this **pattern**: 4, 6, 8, ___, 12?

I Have, Who Has?: Math • 1–2 © 2007 Creative Teaching Press

Patterns — Game B

I have **10**.

Who has the missing
number in this **pattern**:
3, 5, 7, ___, 11?

I have **25**.

Who has the missing
number in this **pattern**:
50, 45, 40, ___, 30?

I have **9**.

Who has the missing
number in this **pattern**:
49, 59, 69, ___, 89?

I have **35**.

Who has the missing
number in this **pattern**:
50, 55, 60, ___, 70?

I have **79**.

Who has the missing
number in this **pattern**:
20, 40, 60, ___, 100?

I have **65**.

Who has the missing
number in this **pattern**:
52, 62, 72, ___, 92?

I have **80**.

Who has the missing
number in this **pattern**:
10, 15, 20, ___, 30?

I have **82**.

Who has the **first card**?

I Have, Who Has?: Math • 1–2 © 2007 Creative Teaching Press

Patterns — Game B

I Lightly color each number that matches your classmates' answers.

1	2	3	4	5	6	7	8	9	10
11	12	13	14	15	16	17	18	19	20
21	22	23	24	25	26	27	28	29	30
31	32	33	34	35	36	37	38	39	40
41	42	43	44	45	46	47	48	49	50
51	52	53	54	55	56	57	58	59	60
61	62	63	64	65	66	67	68	69	70
71	72	73	74	75	76	77	78	79	80
81	82	83	84	85	86	87	88	89	90
91	92	93	94	95	96	97	98	99	100

II Choose 2 numbers from the hundred chart that you did **not** color. Create 2 **different patterns** using each of those numbers **as the missing number**. Then, trade with a partner to solve it.

My Number Pattern	My Number Pattern Solved By: _____

Guess My Number

I have the **first card**.

Who has the **even number that is greater than 97 but less than 100?**

I have **21**.

Who has the **even number that is greater than 19 but less than 22?**

I have **98**.

Who has the **odd number that is greater than 54 but less than 57?**

I have **20**.

Who has the **odd number that is greater than 59 but less than 63?**

I have **55**.

Who has the **even number that is greater than 25 but less than 28?**

I have **61**.

Who has the **even number that is greater than 6 but less than 10?**

I have **26**.

Who has the **odd number that is greater than 20 but less than 23?**

I have **8**.

Who has the **odd number that is greater than 21 but less than 25?**

I Have, Who Has?: Math • 1–2 © 2007 Creative Teaching Press

Guess My Number

I have **23**.

Who has the **even number that is greater than 46 but less than 50?**

I have **79**.

Who has the **even number that has 2 tens and is greater than 26?**

I have **48**.

Who has the **odd number that is greater than 79 but less than 83?**

I have **28**.

Who has the **odd number that has 5 tens and is greater than 57?**

I have **81**.

Who has the **even number that has 3 tens and is greater than 36?**

I have **59**.

Who has the **even number that has 9 tens and is less than 92?**

I have **38**.

Who has the **odd number that has 7 tens and is greater than 77?**

I have **90**.

Who has the **odd number that has 7 tens and is less than 73?**

Guess My Number

I have **71**.

Who has the **even number that has 8 tens and is greater than 86?**

I have **41**.

Who has the **even number that has 9 tens and is between 92 and 96?**

I have **88**.

Who has the **odd number that has 1 ten and is less than 13?**

I have **94**.

Who has the **odd number that has 7 tens and is less than 75 but more than 71?**

I have **11**.

Who has the **even number that has 5 tens and is greater than 56?**

I have **73**.

Who has the number that **has 9 ones and is greater than 89 but less than 100?**

I have **58**.

Who has the **odd number that has 4 tens and is less than 43?**

I have **99**.

Who has the number that **has 2 ones and is between 60 and 70?**

I Have, Who Has?: Math • 1–2 © 2007 Creative Teaching Press

Guess My Number

I have **62**.

Who has the number that **has 6 ones and is between 75 and 85**?

I have **6**.

Who has the **odd number that has 2 more tens than 57**?

I have **76**.

Who has the number that **has 0 ones and is between 40 and 60**?

I have **77**.

Who has the **odd number that has 4 fewer tens than 83**?

I have **50**.

Who has the **odd number that is between 2 and 5**?

I have **43**.

Who has the **odd number that has 2 fewer tens than 57**?

I have **3**.

Who has the **even number that is between 5 and 8**?

I have **37**.

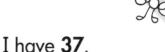

Who has the **first card**?

I Have, Who Has? Math • 1–2 © 2007 Creative Teaching Press

Name _____ Date _____

Guess My Number

I Lightly color each number that matches your classmates' answers.

1	2	3	4	5	6	7	8	9	10
11	12	13	14	15	16	17	18	19	20
21	22	23	24	25	26	27	28	29	30
31	32	33	34	35	36	37	38	39	40
41	42	43	44	45	46	47	48	49	50
51	52	53	54	55	56	57	58	59	60
61	62	63	64	65	66	67	68	69	70
71	72	73	74	75	76	77	78	79	80
81	82	83	84	85	86	87	88	89	90
91	92	93	94	95	96	97	98	99	100

II Choose 2 numbers from the hundred chart that you did **not** color. Write **2 clues** for each number. Trade with a partner to solve. (Remember to cover the numbers first.)

Number from the 100 Chart	My Clues

I Have, Who Has?: Math • 1–2 © 2007 Creative Teaching Press

Place Value — Game A

I have the **first card**.

Who has the number equal
to **5 tens and 3 ones**?

I have **65**.

Who has the number equal
to **3 tens and 5 ones**?

I have **53**.

Who has the number equal
to **3 tens and 2 ones**?

I have **35**.

Who has the number equal
to **2 tens and 1 one**?

I have **32**.

Who has the number equal
to **4 tens and 7 ones**?

I have **21**.

Who has the number equal
to **5 tens and 9 ones**?

I have **47**.

Who has the number equal
to **6 tens and 5 ones**?

I have **59**.

Who has the number equal
to **9 tens and 8 ones**?

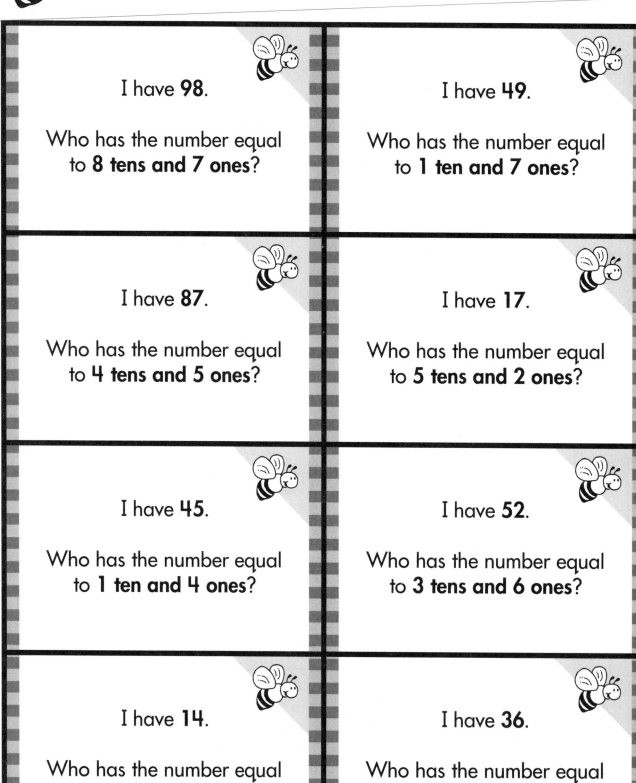

I have **98**.

Who has the number equal to **8 tens and 7 ones**?

I have **49**.

Who has the number equal to **1 ten and 7 ones**?

I have **87**.

Who has the number equal to **4 tens and 5 ones**?

I have **17**.

Who has the number equal to **5 tens and 2 ones**?

I have **45**.

Who has the number equal to **1 ten and 4 ones**?

I have **52**.

Who has the number equal to **3 tens and 6 ones**?

I have **14**.

Who has the number equal to **4 tens and 9 ones**?

I have **36**.

Who has the number equal to **8 tens and 4 ones**?

I Have, Who Has?: Math • 1–2 © 2007 Creative Teaching Press

Place Value — Game A

I have **84**.

Who has the number equal to **3 tens and 0 ones**?

I have **44**.

Who has the number equal to **1 ten and 0 ones**?

I have **30**.

Who has the number equal to **0 tens and 6 ones**?

I have **10**.

Who has the number equal to **0 tens and 1 one**?

I have **6**.

Who has the number equal to **5 tens and 5 ones**?

I have **1**.

Who has the number equal to **6 tens and 6 ones**?

I have **55**.

Who has the number equal to **4 tens and 4 ones**?

I have **66**.

Who has the number equal to **8 tens and 0 ones**?

Place Value — Game A

I have **80**.

Who has the number equal
to **4 tens and 6 ones**?

I have **51**.

Who has the number equal
to **9 tens and 3 ones**?

I have **46**.

Who has the number equal
to **0 tens and 8 ones**?

I have **93**.

Who has the number equal
to **6 tens and 2 ones**?

I have **8**.

Who has the number equal
to **4 tens and 8 ones**?

I have **62**.

Who has the number equal
to **5 tens and 0 ones**?

I have **48**.

Who has the number equal
to **5 tens and 1 one**?

I have **50**.

Who has the **first card**?

I Have, Who Has?: Math • 1–2 © 2007 Creative Teaching Press

Name _____ Date _____

Place Value — Game A

I Lightly color each number that matches your classmates' answers.

1	2	3	4	5	6	7	8	9	10
11	12	13	14	15	16	17	18	19	20
21	22	23	24	25	26	27	28	29	30
31	32	33	34	35	36	37	38	39	40
41	42	43	44	45	46	47	48	49	50
51	52	53	54	55	56	57	58	59	60
61	62	63	64	65	66	67	68	69	70
71	72	73	74	75	76	77	78	79	80
81	82	83	84	85	86	87	88	89	90
91	92	93	94	95	96	97	98	99	100

II Choose 5 numbers from the hundred chart that you did **not** color. Write the **tens** and **ones** for each number. The first one has been done for you.

Number from the 100 Chart	28				
Tens and Ones	2 tens 8 ones				

Place Value — Game B

I have the **first card**.

Who has the sum of
**5 tens and 3 ones +
2 tens and 3 ones?**

I have **4 tens and 5 ones**.

Who has the sum of
**1 ten and 0 ones +
0 tens and 9 ones?**

I have **7 tens and 6 ones**.

Who has the sum of
**2 tens and 0 ones +
2 tens and 1 one?**

I have **1 ten and 9 ones**.

Who has the sum of
**3 tens and 2 ones +
2 tens and 2 ones?**

I have **4 tens and 1 one**.

Who has the sum of
**4 tens and 2 ones +
3 tens and 7 ones?**

I have **5 tens and 4 ones**.

Who has the sum of
**7 tens and 3 ones +
2 tens and 1 one?**

I have **7 tens and 9 ones**.

Who has the sum of
**2 tens and 4 ones +
2 tens and 1 one?**

I have **9 tens and 4 ones**.

Who has the sum of
**1 ten and 3 ones +
1 ten and 2 ones?**

I Have, Who Has?: Math • 1–2 © 2007 Creative Teaching Press

I have **2 tens and 5 ones**.

Who has the sum of
**4 tens and 2 ones +
3 tens and 2 ones**?

I have **2 tens and 0 ones**.

Who has the sum of
**5 tens and 6 ones +
2 tens and 1 one**?

I have **7 tens and 4 ones**.

Who has the sum of
**7 tens and 5 ones +
2 tens and 4 ones**?

I have **7 tens and 7 ones**.

Who has the sum of
**3 tens and 2 ones +
2 tens and 0 ones**?

I have **9 tens and 9 ones**.

Who has the sum of
**2 tens and 3 ones +
0 tens and 3 ones**?

I have **5 tens and 2 ones**.

Who has the sum of
**2 tens and 2 ones +
1 ten and 2 ones**?

I have **2 tens and 6 ones**.

Who has the sum of
**1 ten and 0 ones +
1 ten and 0 ones**?

I have **3 tens and 4 ones**.

Who has the sum of
**1 ten and 1 one +
0 tens and 6 ones**?

I Have, Who Has?: Math • 1–2 © 2007 Creative Teaching Press

Place Value — Game B

I have **1 ten and 7 ones**.

Who has the sum of
**5 tens and 0 ones +
2 tens and 0 ones**?

I have **9 tens and 7 ones**.

Who has the sum of
**2 tens and 2 ones +
1 ten and 0 ones**?

I have **7 tens and 0 ones**.

Who has the sum of
**6 tens and 1 one +
2 tens and 0 ones**?

I have **3 tens and 2 ones**.

Who has the sum of
**3 tens and 0 ones +
2 tens and 0 ones**?

I have **8 tens and 1 one**.

Who has the sum of
**1 ten and 2 ones +
0 tens and 2 ones**?

I have **5 tens and 0 ones**.

Who has the sum of
**4 tens and 1 one +
3 tens and 1 one**?

I have **1 ten and 4 ones**.

Who has the sum of
**5 tens and 5 ones +
4 tens and 2 ones**?

I have **7 tens and 2 ones**.

Who has the sum of
**3 tens and 3 ones +
2 tens and 2 ones**?

I Have, Who Has?: Math • 1–2 © 2007 Creative Teaching Press

Place Value — Game B

I have **5 tens and 5 ones**.

Who has the sum of
**1 ten and 1 one +
1 ten and 0 ones**?

I have **4 tens and 6 ones**.

Who has the sum of
**3 tens and 6 ones +
2 tens and 1 one**?

I have **2 tens and 1 one**.

Who has the sum of
**2 tens and 0 ones +
1 ten and 0 ones**?

I have **5 tens and 7 ones**.

Who has the sum of
**4 tens and 3 ones +
3 tens and 2 ones**?

I have **3 tens and 0 ones**.

Who has the sum of
**1 ten and 0 ones +
0 tens and 2 ones**?

I have **7 tens and 5 ones**.

Who has the sum of
**6 tens and 2 ones +
3 tens and 0 ones**?

I have **1 ten and 2 ones**.

Who has the sum of
**2 tens and 3 ones +
2 tens and 3 ones**?

I have **9 tens and 2 ones**.

Who has the **first card**?

Name _____ Date _____

Place Value — Game B

I Finish the maze by lightly coloring the tens and ones as your classmates say them.

*Start	7 tens 6 ones	4 tens 1 one	7 tens 9 ones
2 tens 6 ones	9 tens 9 ones	3 tens 0 ones	4 tens 5 ones
2 tens 0 ones	7 tens 4 ones	2 tens 5 ones	1 ten 9 ones
7 tens 7 ones	5 tens 2 ones	9 tens 4 ones	5 tens 4 ones
2 tens 4 ones	3 tens 4 ones	4 tens 7 ones	4 tens 5 ones
6 tens 4 ones	1 ten 7 ones	7 tens 0 ones	8 tens 1 one
3 tens 0 ones	2 tens 1 one	2 tens 2 ones	1 ten 4 ones
1 ten 2 ones	5 tens 5 ones	7 tens 2 ones	9 tens 7 ones
4 tens 6 ones	5 tens 7 ones	5 tens 0 ones	3 tens 2 ones
1 ten 1 one	7 tens 5 ones	9 tens 2 ones	*Finish
A	**B**	**C**	**D**

II Look at the boxes in columns **A** and **C** that you did **not** color. Write the **tens** and **ones** from each box below. Add each set of three numbers together. How many tens and ones are in each answer?

Column A

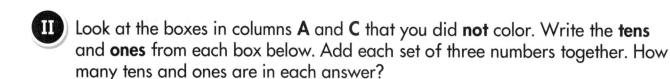

____ tens ____ ones + ____ tens ____ ones + ____ ten ____ one = ____ tens ____ ones

Column C

____ tens ____ ones + ____ tens ____ ones + ____ tens ____ ones = ____ tens ____ ones

I Have, Who Has?: Math • 1–2 © 2007 Creative Teaching Press

Place Value — Game C

I have the **first card**.

Who has the number with
5 tens that is greater than 58?

I have **40**.

Who has the number with
**2 tens that is between
24 and 26?**

I have **59**.

Who has the number with
7 tens that is less than 71?

I have **25**.

Who has the number with
7 tens that is greater than 78?

I have **70**.

Who has the number with
3 tens that is greater than 38?

I have **79**.

Who has the number with
1 ten that is less than 11?

I have **39**.

Who has the number with
4 tens that is less than 41?

I have **10**.

Who has the number with
**6 tens that is between
63 and 65?**

Place Value — Game C

I have **64**.

Who has the number with
9 tens that is greater than 98?

I have **95**.

Who has the numbers with
2 ones that are less than 20?

I have **99**.

Who has the number with
8 tens that is less than 81?

I have **2 and 12**.

Who has the number with
**7 ones that is between
90 and 100?**

I have **80**.

Who has the number with
**7 tens that is between
73 and 75?**

I have **97**.

Who has the number with
3 ones that is less than 10?

I have **74**.

Who has the number with
**5 ones that is between
86 and 100?**

I have **3**.

Who has the numbers with
9 ones that are less than 20?

Place Value — Game C

I have **9 and 19**.

Who has the number with
**6 ones that is between
88 and 98?**

I have **1**.

Who has the number with
**6 ones that is between
50 and 60?**

I have **96**.

Who has the number with
**4 ones that is between
40 and 50?**

I have **56**.

Who has the number with
**1 one that is between
85 and 100?**

I have **44**.

Who has the number with
**8 ones that is between
80 and 90?**

I have **91**.

Who has the numbers with
**7 tens that are between
75 and 78?**

I have **88**.

Who has the number with
1 one that is less than 10?

I have **76 and 77**.

Who has the number that is
**1 ten more than 3 tens
and 2 ones?**

Place Value — Game C

I have **42**.

Who has the number that is
**4 tens more than 2 tens
and 7 ones?**

I have **29**.

Who has the number that is
**5 tens more than 0 tens
and 7 ones?**

I have **67**.

Who has the number that is
**3 tens less than 9 tens
and 3 ones?**

I have **57**.

Who has the number that is
**4 tens less than 4 tens
and 7 ones?**

I have **63**.

Who has the number that is
**2 tens less than 7 tens
and 5 ones?**

I have **7**.

Who has the number that is
**3 tens more than 1 ten
and 5 ones?**

I have **55**.

Who has the number that is
**6 tens less than 8 tens
and 9 ones?**

I have **45**.

Who has the **first card**?

I Have, Who Has?: Math • 1–2 © 2007 Creative Teaching Press

Place Value — Game C

I Lightly color each number that matches your classmates' answers.

1	2	3	4	5	6	7	8	9	10
11	12	13	14	15	16	17	18	19	20
21	22	23	24	25	26	27	28	29	30
31	32	33	34	35	36	37	38	39	40
41	42	43	44	45	46	47	48	49	50
51	52	53	54	55	56	57	58	59	60
61	62	63	64	65	66	67	68	69	70
71	72	73	74	75	76	77	78	79	80
81	82	83	84	85	86	87	88	89	90
91	92	93	94	95	96	97	98	99	100

II Choose 2 numbers from the hundred chart that you did **not** color. Write **2 place value clues** for each. Trade with a partner to solve. (Remember to cover the numbers first.)

Number from the Hundred Chart	My Place Value Clues

Place Value — Game D

I have the **first card**.

Who has the **sum of
22 + 38**?

I have **61**.

Who has the **sum of
58 + 6**?

I have **60**.

Who has the **sum of
15 + 15**?

I have **64**.

Who has the **sum of
29 + 11**?

I have **30**.

Who has the **sum of
17 + 4**?

I have **40**.

Who has the **sum of
25 + 25**?

I have **21**.

Who has the **sum of
26 + 35**?

I have **50**.

Who has the **sum of
27 + 24**?

I Have, Who Has?: Math • 1–2 © 2007 Creative Teaching Press

Place Value — Game D

I have **51**.

Who has the **sum of**
35 + 35?

I have **52**.

Who has the **sum of**
22 + 19?

I have **70**.

Who has the **sum of**
35 + 36?

I have **41**.

Who has the **sum of**
19 + 17?

I have **71**.

Who has the **sum of**
18 + 15?

I have **36**.

Who has the **sum of**
69 + 12?

I have **33**.

Who has the **sum of**
37 + 15?

I have **81**.

Who has the **sum of**
47 + 33?

I Have, Who Has?, Math • 1–2 © 2007 Creative Teaching Press

Place Value — Game D

I have **80**.

Who has the **sum of**
17 + 14?

I have **93**.

Who has the **sum of**
16 + 16?

I have **31**.

Who has the **sum of**
54 + 28?

I have **32**.

Who has the **sum of**
18 + 16?

I have **82**.

Who has the **sum of**
79 + 12?

I have **34**.

Who has the **sum of**
38 + 15?

I have **91**.

Who has the **sum of**
78 + 15?

I have **53**.

Who has the **sum of**
57 + 9?

Place Value — Game D

I have **66**.

Who has the **sum of
39 + 26**?

I have **37**.

Who has the **sum of
28 + 48**?

I have **65**.

Who has the **sum of
77 + 13**?

I have **76**.

Who has the **sum of
46 + 54**?

I have **90**.

Who has the **sum of
58 + 25**?

I have **100**.

Who has the **sum of
38 + 36**?

I have **83**.

Who has the **sum of
19 + 18**?

I have **74**.

Who has the **first card**?

I Have, Who Has?: Math • 1–2 © 2007 Creative Teaching Press

Name _____ Date _____

Place Value — Game D

I Lightly color each number that matches your classmates' answers.

1	2	3	4	5	6	7	8	9	10
11	12	13	14	15	16	17	18	19	20
21	22	23	24	25	26	27	28	29	30
31	32	33	34	35	36	37	38	39	40
41	42	43	44	45	46	47	48	49	50
51	52	53	54	55	56	57	58	59	60
61	62	63	64	65	66	67	68	69	70
71	72	73	74	75	76	77	78	79	80
81	82	83	84	85	86	87	88	89	90
91	92	93	94	95	96	97	98	99	100

II Add the numbers by regrouping.

1. $\begin{array}{r} 32 \\ + 68 \\ \hline \end{array}$

2. $\begin{array}{r} 19 \\ + 23 \\ \hline \end{array}$

3. $\begin{array}{r} 77 \\ + 4 \\ \hline \end{array}$

4. $\begin{array}{r} 21 \\ + 29 \\ \hline \end{array}$

Time — Game A

I have the **first card**.

Who has the **name of the hand on the clock that is the longest?**

I have **30 minutes**.

Who has the **number of hours in a day?**

I have the **minute hand**.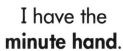

Who has the **name of the hand on the clock that is the shortest?**

I have **24 hours**.

Who has what we write after the times that come **after midnight but before noon?**

I have the **hour hand**.

Who has the **number of minutes in an hour?**

I have **a.m.**

Who has what we write after the times that come **after noon but before midnight?**

I have **60 minutes**.

Who has the **number of minutes in a half hour?**

I have **p.m.**

Who has the time when the **hour hand is on the 8 and the minute hand goes straight up?**

Time — Game A

I have **8:00**.

Who has the time when
the **hour hand is on the 3
and the minute hand goes
straight up**?

I have **9:00**.

Who has the time when
the **hour hand is on the 12
and the minute hand goes
straight up**?

I have **3:00**.

Who has the time when
the **hour hand is on the 5
and the minute hand goes
straight up**?

I have **12:00**.

Who has the time when
the **hour hand is just past
the 2 and the minute hand
goes straight down**?

I have **5:00**.

Who has the time when
the **hour hand is on the 6
and the minute hand goes
straight up**?

I have **2:30**.

Who has the time when
the **hour hand is just past
the 4 and the minute hand
goes straight down**?

I have **6:00**.

Who has the time when
the **hour hand is on the 9
and the minute hand goes
straight up**?

I have **4:30**.

Who has the time when
the **hour hand is just past the
6 and the minute hand goes
straight down**?

Time — Game A

I have **6:30**.

Who has the time that is
one hour past 1:00?

I have **10:00**.

Who has the time that is
one hour after 4:30?

I have **2:00**.

Who has the time that is
one hour before 12:00?

I have **5:30**.

Who has the time that is
a half hour before 10:00?

I have **11:00**.

Who has the time that is
one hour past 6:00?

I have **9:30**.

Who has the time that is
a half hour after 10:00?

I have **7:00**.

Who has the time that is
one hour before 11:00?

I have **10:30**.

Who has the time that is
a half hour before 8:00?

Time — Game A

I have **7:30**.

Who has the time that is
a half hour past 8:00?

I have **3:30**.

Who has the time that is
a half hour past 1:00?

I have **8:30**.

Who has the time that is
a half hour before 4:30?

I have **1:30**.

Who has the time that is
a half hour before 1:00?

I have **4:00**.

Who has the time that is
a half hour after 12:30?

I have **12:30**.

Who has the time that is
a half hour before 12:00?

I have **1:00**.

Who has the time that is
a half hour before 4:00?

I have **11:30**.

Who has the **first card**?

I Have, Who Has?: Math • 1–2 © 2007 Creative Teaching Press

Time — Game A

I Finish the maze by lightly coloring the boxes that match your classmates' answers.

*Start	long hand	11:00	7:00	3:30	1:30
minute hand	short hand	2:00	10:00	5:30	9:30
hour hand	60 minutes	6:30	4:30	7:30	10:30
24 hours	30 minutes	3:00	2:30	8:30	2:00
a.m.	p.m.	5:00	12:00	4:00	12:00
7:30	8:00	11:00	9:00	1:00	3:30
2:30	3:00	5:00	6:00	12:30	1:30
4:30	6:30	2:00	11:00	11:30	***Finish**

II Choose 3 of the times written in the chart above that you did **not** color. Mark the hands on the clocks below to show each of those times.

Example:

   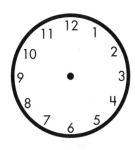

Time — Game B

I have the **first card**.

Who has the **time that is one hour past 3:30?**

I have **5:45**.

Who has the **time that is a half hour past 12:30?**

I have **4:30**.

Who has the **time that is one hour before 1:00?**

I have **1:00**.

Who has the **time that is a half hour before 1:00?**

I have **12:00**.

Who has the **time that is one hour after 7:15?**

I have **12:30**.

Who has the **time that is a half hour after 1:30?**

I have **8:15**.

Who has the **time that is one hour before 6:45?**

I have **2:00**.

Who has the **time that is a half hour before 11:00?**

I Have, Who Has?: Math • 1–2 © 2007 Creative Teaching Press

Time — Game B

I have **10:30**.

Who has the **time that is a half hour past 4:45?**

I have **11:15**.

Who has the **time that is a half hour past 2:45?**

I have **5:15**.

Who has the **time that is a half hour before 3:15?**

I have **3:15**.

Who has the **time that is 15 minutes after 6:30?**

I have **2:45**.

Who has the **time that is a half hour after 3:15?**

I have **6:45**.

Who has the **time that is 15 minutes before 8:00?**

I have **3:45**.

Who has the **time that is a half hour before 11:45?**

I have **7:45**.

Who has the **time that is 15 minutes past 10:00?**

Time — Game B

I have **10:15**.

Who has the **time that is
15 minutes before 5:00**?

I have **9:30**.

Who has the **time that is
15 minutes before 1:00**?

I have **4:45**.

Who has the **time that is
15 minutes after 6:00**?

I have **12:45**.

Who has the **time that is
15 minutes after 9:45**?

I have **6:15**.

Who has the **time that is
15 minutes before 1:45**?

I have **10:00**.

Who has the **time that is
15 minutes before 4:15**?

I have **1:30**.

Who has the **time that is
15 minutes past 9:15**?

I have **4:00**.

Who has the **time that is
15 minutes past 6:45**?

I Have, Who Has?: Math • 1–2 © 2007 Creative Teaching Press

Time — Game B

I have **7:00**.

Who has the **time that is 45 minutes after 8:00**?

I have **4:15**.

Who has the **time that is 45 minutes after 12:30**?

I have **8:45**.

Who has the **time that is 45 minutes after 11:00**?

I have **1:15**.

Who has the **time that is 45 minutes past 2:15**?

I have **11:45**.

Who has the **time that is 45 minutes after 6:30**?

I have **3:00**.

Who has the **time that is 45 minutes after 6:45**?

I have **7:15**.

Who has the **time that is 45 minutes after 3:30**?

I have **7:30**.

Who has the **first card**?

Name _____ Date _____

Time — Game B

I Write each time from left to right as your classmates say the answers.

*Start →			

II Choose 6 of the times written in the chart above. Mark the hands on the clocks below to show each of those times.

Example:

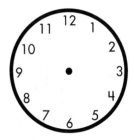

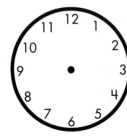

Time — Game C

Note: Make a copy of the Calendar Reproducible (page 162) on an overhead transparency. Display the transparency while students play the game.

I have the **first card**.

Who has the **number of days in a week**?

I have **Sunday**.

Who has the **day of the week that comes after Tuesday**?

I have **7 days**.

Who has the **number of months in a year**?

I have **Wednesday**.

Who has the **day of the week that comes before Sunday**?

I have **12 months**.

Who has the **number of seasons in a year**?

I have **Saturday**.

Who has the **day of the week that comes after Thursday**?

I have **4 seasons**.

Who has the **day of the week that comes before Monday**?

I have **Friday**.

Who has the **day of the week that comes before Wednesday**?

Time — Game C

I have **Tuesday**.

Who has the **day of the week that comes after Sunday**?

I have **August**.

Who has the **month that comes after January**?

I have **Monday**.

Who has the **day of the week that comes before Friday**?

I have **February**.

Who has the **month that comes before December**?

I have **Thursday**.

Who has the **month that comes before July**?

I have **November**.

Who has the **month that comes after March**?

I have **June**.

Who has the **month that comes after July**?

I have **April**.

Who has the **month that comes after August**?

I Have, Who Has?: Math • 1–2 © 2007 Creative Teaching Press

Time — Game C

I have **September**.

Who has the **month that comes before June?**

I have **December**.

Who has the **month that comes before August?**

I have **May**.

Who has the **month that comes after December?**

I have **July**.

Who has the **month that comes after September?**

I have **January**.

Who has the **month that comes before April?**

I have **October**.

Who has the **last day in July?**

I have **March**.

Who has the **month that comes after November?**

I have the **31ˢᵗ**.

Who has the **second Saturday in July?**

I Have, Who Has?: Math • 1–2 © 2007 Creative Teaching Press

Time — Game C

I have the **8**th.

Who has the **second Tuesday in July**?

I have the **15**th.

Who has the **second Monday in July**?

I have the **11**th.

Who has the **first Monday in July**?

I have the **10**th.

Who has the **third Thursday in July**?

I have the **3**rd.

Who has the **second Thursday in July**?

I have the **20**th.

Who has the **fourth Saturday in July**?

I have the **13**th.

Who has the **third Saturday in July**?

I have the **22**nd.

Who has the **first card**?

Name _____ Date _____

Time — Game C

I Lightly color the boxes to finish the maze as your classmates use the calendar to find the answers.

*Start	4 seasons	Sunday	Tuesday	2nd	30th
7 days	12 months	Wednesday	Thursday	12th	24th
10th	Friday	Saturday	October	4th	26th
Monday	Tuesday	February	November	1st	29th
Thursday	June	August	April	15th	10th
Friday	Wednesday	May	September	13th	20th
December	March	January	November	3rd	22nd
July	October	31st	8th	11th	***Finish**

II Use the calendar to answer the following questions.

1. Write the days of the week in order. _____

_____

2. How many days are in 1 week? _____ 2 weeks? _____

3. How many Saturdays are in July on the calendar? _____

4. How many Mondays are in July on the calendar? _____

5. What is the date on the last day in July on the calendar? _____

Time — Game C
Overhead Transparency
July

Sunday	Monday	Tuesday	Wednesday	Thursday	Friday	Saturday
						1
2	3	4	5	6	7	8
9	10	11	12	13	14	15
16	17	18	19	20	21	22
23 / 30	24 / 31	25	26	27	28	29

Money — Game A

I have the **first card**.

Who has the **name of the coin worth 1 cent**?

I have a **quarter**.

Who has the **name of the coin worth 50 cents**?

I have a **penny**.

Who has the **name of the coin worth 5 cents**?

I have a **half dollar**.

Who has the **name of the coin worth 100 cents**?

I have a **nickel**.

Who has the **name of the coin worth 10 cents**?

I have a **dollar**.

Who has the **value of a quarter**?

I have a **dime**.

Who has the **name of the coin worth 25 cents**?

I have **25¢**.

Who has the **value of a dime**?

Money — Game A

I have **10¢**.

Who has the **value of
a dollar**?

I have **5¢**.

Who has the **2 coins worth
the same as 1 dime**?

I have **100¢**.

Who has the **value of
a penny**?

I have **2 nickels**.

Who has the **10 coins worth
the same as 1 dollar**?

I have **1 ¢**.

Who has the **value of
a half dollar**?

I have **10 dimes**.

Who has the **5 coins worth
the same as 1 quarter**?

I have **50¢**.

Who has the **value of
a nickel**?

I have **5 nickels**.

Who has the **4 coins worth
the same as 1 dollar**?

I Have, Who Has?: Math • 1–2 © 2007 Creative Teaching Press

Money — Game A

I have **4 quarters**.

Who has the **2 coins worth the same as 1 dollar**?

I have **25 pennies**.

Who has the **3 coins worth the same as 1 quarter**?

I have **2 half dollars**.

Who has the **2 coins worth the same as 1 half dollar**?

I have **2 dimes and 1 nickel**.

Who has the **value of 1 quarter + 1 nickel**?

I have **2 quarters**.

Who has the **5 coins worth the same as 2 quarters**?

I have **30¢**

Who has the **value of 1 quarter + 3 pennies**?

I have **5 dimes**.

Who has the **25 coins worth the same as 1 quarter**?

I have **28¢**.

Who has the **value of 1 quarter + 1 dime**?

Money — Game A

I have **35¢**.

Who has the **value of 2 quarters + 1 penny**?

I have **17¢**.

Who has the **value of 1 dime + 1 nickel**?

I have **51¢**.

Who has the **value of 2 quarters + 3 dimes**?

I have **15¢**.

Who has the **value of 4 dimes + 1 nickel**?

I have **80¢**.

Who has the **value of 3 quarters**?

I have **45¢**.

Who has the **value of 4 nickels + 2 pennies**?

I have **75¢**.

Who has the **value of 1 dime + 7 pennies**?

I have **22¢**.

Who has the **first card**?

I Have, Who Has?: Math • 1–2 © 2007 Creative Teaching Press

Name _____ Date _____

Money — Game A

I Finish the maze by lightly coloring the boxes that match your classmates' answers.

*Start	55¢	10¢	100¢	1¢	50¢
penny	35¢	25¢	dollar	2 nickels	5¢
nickel	dime	quarter	half dollar	10 dimes	5 nickels
75¢	30¢	2 dimes and 1 nickel	25 pennies	5 dimes	4 quarters
17¢	28¢	60¢	5 dollars	2 quarters	2 half dollars
51¢	35¢	38¢	79¢	40¢	27¢
80¢	75¢	17¢	85¢	99¢	65¢
84¢	44¢	15¢	45¢	22¢	***Finish**

II Choose 4 amounts that you did **not** color. Write **2 different ways to show that amount**. An example has been done for you.

Amount	First Way to Make It	Second Way to Make It
17¢	1 dime + 7 pennies	3 nickels + 2 pennies

I Have, Who Has?: Math • 1–2 © 2007 Creative Teaching Press

Money — Game B

I have the **first card**.

Who has the **value of**
1 dollar + 2 quarters?

I have **$2.00**.

Who has the **value of**
1 dollar + 3 dimes?

I have **$1.50**.

Who has the **value of**
1 dollar + 2 dimes?

I have **$1.30**.

Who has the **value of**
1 dollar + 3 nickels?

I have **$1.20**.

Who has the **value of**
1 dollar + 2 pennies?

I have **$1.15**.

Who has the **value of**
1 dollar + 3 quarters?

I have **$1.02**.

Who has the **value of**
1 dollar + 2 half dollars?

I have **$1.75**.

Who has the **value of**
1 dollar + 5 nickels?

I Have, Who Has?: Math • 1–2 © 2007 Creative Teaching Press

Money — Game B

I have **$1.25**.

Who has the **value of
1 dollar + 7 dimes**?

I have **$1.01**.

Who has the **value of
6 quarters + 1 penny**?

I have **$1.70**.

Who has the **value of
4 quarters + 1 dime**?

I have **$1.51**.

Who has the **value of
6 quarters + 1 dime**?

I have **$1.10**.

Who has the **value of
4 quarters + 1 nickel**?

I have **$1.60**.

Who has the **value of
6 quarters + 1 nickel**?

I have **$1.05**.

Who has the **value of
4 quarters + 1 penny**?

I have **$1.55**.

Who has the **value of
5 quarters + 1 dime**?

Money — Game B

I have **$1.35**.

Who has the **value of 5 quarters + 2 dimes**?

I have **$2.75**.

Who has the **value of 2 dollars + 5 nickels**?

I have **$1.45**.

Who has the **value of 8 quarters + 1 half dollar**?

I have **$2.25**.

Who has the **value of 1 dollar + 1 quarter + 1 penny**?

I have **$2.50**.

Who has the **value of 2 dollars + 4 dimes**?

I have **$1.26**.

Who has the **value of 1 dollar + 1 dime + 1 penny**?

I have **$2.40**.

Who has the **value of 2 dollars + 3 quarters**?

I have **$1.11**.

Who has the **value of 1 dollar + 1 nickel + 4 pennies**?

Money — Game B

 I have **$1.09**.

Who has the **value of 1 dollar + 2 quarters + 3 nickels**?

 I have **$1.58**.

Who has the **value of 1 dollar + 3 quarters + 2 dimes**?

 I have **$1.65**.

Who has the **value of 1 dollar + 3 quarters + 1 nickel**?

I have **$1.95**.

Who has the **value of 8 dimes + 4 nickels**?

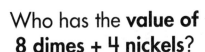 I have **$1.80**.

Who has the **value of 1 dollar + 3 quarters + 1 dime**?

 I have **$1.00**.

Who has the **value of 1 dollar + 3 quarters + 3 nickels**?

I have **$1.85**.

Who has the **value of 1 dollar + 1 half dollar + 8 pennies**?

 I have **$1.90**.

Who has the **first card**?

Money — Game B

I Write each money value from left to right as your classmates say the answers.

*Start →			

II Choose 1 amount from each column. Write **2 different ways to show that amount**.

Amount	First Way to Make It	Second Way to Make It

I Have, Who Has?: Math • 1–2 © 2007 Creative Teaching Press

Units of Length, Capacity, Weight, and Time

I have the **first card**.

Who has the **name of what is measured in inches or feet?**

I have **weight**.

Who has the **number of inches in a foot?**

I have **length**.

Who has the **name of what is measured in cups or gallons?**

I have **12 inches**.

Who has the **number of inches in a yard?**

I have **capacity**.

Who has the **name of what is measured in days, hours, months, or minutes?**

I have **36 inches**.

Who has the **number of feet in a yard?**

I have **time**.

Who has the **name of what is measured in pounds or ounces?**

I have **3 feet**.

Who has the **number of inches in 2 feet?**

Units of Length, Capacity, Weight, and Time

I have **24 inches**.

Who has the **number of feet in 3 yards**?

I have **4 quarts**.

Who has the **number of pints in a gallon**?

I have **9 feet**.

Who has the **number of cups in a pint**?

I have **8 pints**.

Who has the **number of quarts in 10 gallons**?

I have **2 cups**.

Who has the **number of quarts equal to 4 pints**?

I have **40 quarts**.

Who has the **number of ounces in 1 pound**?

I have **2 quarts**.

Who has the **number of quarts in a gallon**?

I have **16 ounces**.

Who has the **number of seconds in a minute**?

I Have, Who Has?: Math • 1–2 © 2007 Creative Teaching Press

Units of Length, Capacity, Weight, and Time

I have **60 seconds**.

Who has the **number of minutes in a half hour**?

I have **7 days**.

Who has the **number of weeks in a year**?

I have **30 minutes**.

Who has the **number of minutes in a quarter of an hour**?

I have **52 weeks**.

Who has the **number of days in a common year**?

I have **15 minutes**.

Who has the **number of minutes in three quarters of an hour**?

I have **365 days**.

Who has the **word that equals 60 minutes**?

I have **45 minutes**.

Who has the **number of days in a week**?

I have an **hour**.

Who has the **word that equals 12 inches**?

Units of Length, Capacity, Weight, and Time

I have a **foot**.

Who has the **number of inches in half of a foot**?

I have a **year**.

Who has the **word that equals 60 seconds**?

I have **6 inches**.

Who has the **word that equals 24 hours**?

I have a **minute**.

Who has the **word that equals 2 cups**?

I have a **day**.

Who has the **word that equals 7 days**?

I have a **pint**.

Who has the **word that equals 2 pints**?

I have a **week**.

Who has the **word that equals 12 months**?

I have a **quart**.

Who has the **first card**?

I Have, Who Has?: Math • 1–2 © 2007 Creative Teaching Press

Name _____ Date _____

Units of Length, Capacity, Weight, and Time

I Lightly color the boxes as your classmates say the answers to finish the maze.

*Start	length	capacity	time	weight	2 cups	*Finish
2 pints	24 inches	3 feet	36 inches	12 inches	pint	quart
2 cups	9 feet	365 days	hour	foot	minute	60 seconds
2 quarts	4 quarts	52 weeks	7 days	6 inches	year	3 feet
40 quarts	8 pints	15 minutes	45 minutes	day	week	4 quarts
16 ounces	60 seconds	30 minutes	12 inches	60 minutes	365 days	2 pints

II Draw a line from the words on the left to the matching measurement on the right.

1. 12 inches   **a.** one hour

2. 60 minutes   **b.** one pound

3. 365 days   **c.** one day

4. 16 ounces   **d.** one foot

5. 24 hours   **e.** one minute

6. 60 seconds   **f.** one year

7. 3 feet   **g.** one yard

Data Analysis — Game A

Note: Make a copy of the Data Analysis — Game A Reproducible (page 183) on an overhead transparency. Display the transparency while students play the game.

I have the **first card**.

Who has the **name of the graph shaped like a circle?**

I have **horizontal bars**.

Who has the **direction of the bars on the "Favorite Ice Cream Flavors" graph?**

I have a **pie graph**.

Who has the **name of the graph with the bars?**

I have **vertical bars**.

Who has the **total number of people included on the "Most Popular Pets" graph?**

I have a **bar graph**.

Who has the **title of the pie graph?**

I have **23 people**.

Who has the **total number of people included on the "Favorite Ice Cream Flavors" graph?**

I have **"My Normal Weekend Day."**

Who has the **direction of the bars on the "Most Popular Pets" graph?**

I have **25 people**.

Who has the **total number of hours represented on the pie graph?**

I Have, Who Has?: Math • 1–2 © 2007 Creative Teaching Press

Data Analysis — Game A

I have **24 hours**.

Who has the **purpose of the pie graph**?

I have the **guinea pig**.

Who has the **number of people who said the guinea pig was their favorite**?

I have **to show the parts of a whole**.

Who has the **purpose of the bar graph**?

I have **0 people**.

Who has the **number of people who said the rabbit was their favorite**?

I have **to compare different information**.

Who has the **most popular pet**?

I have **6 people**.

Who has the **two animals that were equally popular**?

I have the **dog**.

Who has the **least popular pet**?

I have **rats and hamsters**.

Who has the **animal that is more popular than the cat but less popular than the dog**?

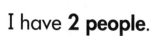

I have the **rabbit**.

Who has **how many more people liked dogs than cats?**

I have **2 people**.

Who has **how much time was spent playing during the day?**

I have **5 people**.

Who has the **most popular ice cream flavor?**

I have **4 hours**.

Who has **how the largest part of the day was spent?**

I have **mint chip**.

Who has the **two flavors that were equally popular?**

I have **sleeping**.

Who has **how the shortest part of the day was spent?**

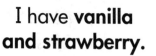

I have **vanilla and strawberry**.

Who has **how many more people liked chocolate chip than chocolate?**

I have **doing chores and eating**.

Who has **how much time was spent on family time?**

I Have, Who Has?: Math • 1–2 © 2007 Creative Teaching Press

Data Analysis — Game A

Favorite Ice Cream Flavors

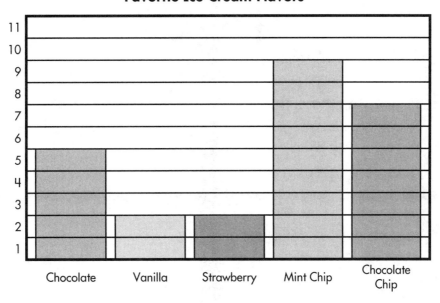

Most Popular Pets

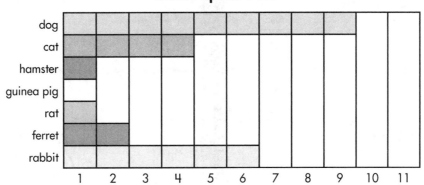

My Normal Weekend Day

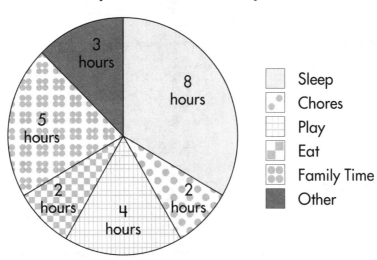

Data Analysis — Game B

Note: Make a copy of the Data Analysis — Game B Reproducible (page 189) on an overhead transparency. Display the transparency while students play the game.

I have the **first card**.

Who has the **value** of the word **go**?

I have **11**.

Who has the **value** of the word **him**?

I have **8**.

Who has the **value** of the word **the**?

I have **21**.

Who has the **value** of the word **you**?

I have **12**.

Who has the **value** of the word **it**?

I have **17**.

Who has the **value** of the word **and**?

I have **13**.

Who has the **value** of the word **man**?

I have **14**.

Who has the **value** of the word **on**?

I have **7**.

Who has the **value** of the word **so**?

I have **16**.

Who has the **value** of the word **get**?

I have **6**.

Who has the **value** of the word **look**?

I have **10**.

Who has the **value** of the word **dad**?

I have **36**.

Who has the **value** of the word **day**?

I have **18**.

Who has the **value** of the word **any**?

I have **19**.

Who has the **value** of the word **may**?

I have **15**.

Who has the **value** of the word **said**?

Data Analysis — Game B

I have **22**.

Who has the **value** of the word **food**?

I have **26**.

Who has the **value** of the word **stop**?

I have **24**.

Who has the **value** of the word **bike**?

I have **20**.

Who has the **value** of the word **after**?

I have **30**.

Who has the **value** of the word **back**?

I have **27**.

Who has the **value** of the word **pick**?

I have **28**.

Who has the **value** of the word **book**?

I have **35**.

Who has the **value** of the word **work**?

I Have, Who Has?: Math • 1–2 © 2007 Creative Teaching Press

Data Analysis — Game B

I have **33**.

Who has the **value** of the word **job**?

I have **34**.

Who has the **value** of the word **like**?

I have **23**.

Who has the **value** of the word **pup**?

I have **40**.

Who has the **value** of the word **happy**?

I have **25**.

Who has the **value** of the word **baby**?

I have **38**.

Who has the **value** of the word **puppy**?

I have **31**.

Who has the **value** of the word **think**?

I have **44**.

Who has the **first card**?

I Have, Who Has?: Math • 1–2 © 2007 Creative Teaching Press

Name _____ Date _____

Data Analysis — Game B

I Write each word value from left to right as your classmates say the answers.

*Start →			
A	**B**	**C**	**D**

II Choose **4** values from column **B**. Create words that are worth that amount using the table.

1. _____

2. _____

3. _____

4. _____

III Use the table to figure out the value of each problem below.

1. your first name _____

2. your last name _____

3. your teacher's name _____

4. your friend's name _____

5. your favorite sport _____

6. your favorite snack _____

I Have, Who Has?: Math • 1–2 © 2007 Creative Teaching Press

Data Analysis — Game B
Overhead Transparency

As your classmates read a word, locate the letters that spell that word in the chart below. Add the values of the letters together to find the total value of the word.

Letter	Value
a	2
b	10
c	6
d	8
e	1
f	10
g	5
h	7
i	9
j	10
k	10
l	20
m	5

Letter	Value
n	4
o	3
p	10
q	20
r	10
s	3
t	4
u	5
v	6
w	10
x	20
y	9
z	20

Word Problems

I have the **first card**.

Who has the answer to this problem? **They had 1 dog and 8 rabbits. How many animals did they have altogether?**

I have **12 birds**.

Who has the answer to this problem? **He read 20 books and 15 magazines. How many books and magazines did he read?**

I have **9 animals**.

Who has the answer to this problem? **She ate 14 berries and 4 bananas. How many pieces of fruit did she eat?**

I have **35 books and magazines**.

Who has the answer to this problem? **He ran 12 miles one day and 20 the next day. How many miles did he run altogether?**

I have **18 pieces**.

Who has the answer to this problem? **He had 4 jackets. Two are missing. How many jackets does he have left?**

I have **32 miles**.

Who has the answer to this problem? **She baked 15 pies and sold 10. How many pies did she have left?**

I have **2 jackets**.

Who has the answer to this problem? **There were 15 birds in a tree. Three flew away. How many birds are in the tree?**

I have **5 pies**.

Who has the answer to this problem? **One box has 6 cups of cereal and the other box has 14 cups. How many cups of cereal are there?**

Word Problems

I have **20 cups**.

Who has the answer to this problem? **There was a school of 50 fish. Twenty swam away. How many fish are left?**

I have **60 cartoons**.

Who has the answer to this problem? **The clown blew up 50 balloons, but 5 popped. How many balloons did not pop?**

I have **30 fish**.

Who has the answer to this problem? **She bought 5 gifts at one store and 10 gifts at another. How many gifts did she buy altogether?**

I have **45 balloons**.

Who has the answer to this problem? **She wrote 12 letters on Monday and 12 on Wednesday. How many letters did she write?**

I have **15 gifts**.

Who has the answer to this problem? **She started with 25 dishes but 2 dishes broke. How many dishes are not broken?**

I have **24 letters**.

Who has the answer to this problem? **He planted 9 tomato plants, but 3 died. How many tomato plants are still alive?**

I have **23 dishes**.

Who has the answer to this problem? **He drew 30 cartoons on Friday and 30 on Saturday. How many cartoons did he draw?**

I have **6 plants**.

Who has the answer to this problem? **He collected 55 bottles to recycle, but 1 fell out along the way. How many bottles were recycled?**

Word Problems

I have **54 bottles**.

Who has the answer to this problem? **He paid 2 bills on Tuesday and 5 on Thursday. How many bills were paid?**

I have **50 cookies**.

Who has the answer to this problem? **A dog buried 11 bones in the front yard and 11 in the backyard. How many bones were buried altogether?**

I have **7 bills**.

Who has the answer to this problem? **The class has 80 markers, but 10 are dried up. How many markers still work?**

I have **22 bones**.

Who has the answer to this problem? **A runner passed 20 boys and 8 girls in the race. How many people did the runner pass?**

I have **70 markers**.

Who has the answer to this problem? **A girl picked 40 apples, but 2 were rotten. How many apples were good to eat?**

I have **28 people**.

Who has the answer to this problem? **There were 12 cookies and 4 cakes for sale. How many desserts were for sale altogether?**

I have **38 apples**.

Who has the answer to this problem? **He baked 25 sugar cookies and 25 peanut butter cookies. How many cookies did he bake altogether?**

I have **16 desserts**.

Who has the answer to this problem? **The store manager had 60 picture frames, but 5 were cracked. How many frames could be sold?**

I Have, Who Has?: Math • 1–2 © 2007 Creative Teaching Press

Word Problems

I have **55 frames**.

Who has the answer to this problem? **There were 30 suckers in a bag. Twenty were eaten. How many suckers are left?**

I have **80 stickers**.

Who has the answer to this problem? **A company had 100 prizes and gave away 25. How many prizes are left?**

I have **10 suckers**.

Who has the answer to this problem? **George bought a pack of 16 batteries. He used 8. How many batteries are left?**

I have **75 prizes**.

Who has the answer to this problem? **There were 30 lightbulbs in the house but 5 were burned out. How many lightbulbs still work?**

I have **8 batteries**.

Who has the answer to this problem? **Mary had a pack of 20 candles. She used 9 candles. How many candles are left?**

I have **25 lightbulbs**.

Who has the answer to this problem? **There were 25 goats and 15 pigs on the farm. How many animals were there?**

I have **11 candles**.

Who has the answer to this problem? **There are 30 stickers in one pack and 50 in the other pack. How many stickers are there altogether?**

I have **40 animals**.

Who has the **first card**?

Name _____ Date _____

Word Problems

I Lightly color each number that matches your classmates' answers.

1	2	3	4	5	6	7	8	9	10
11	12	13	14	15	16	17	18	19	20
21	22	23	24	25	26	27	28	29	30
31	32	33	34	35	36	37	38	39	40
41	42	43	44	45	46	47	48	49	50
51	52	53	54	55	56	57	58	59	60
61	62	63	64	65	66	67	68	69	70
71	72	73	74	75	76	77	78	79	80
81	82	83	84	85	86	87	88	89	90
91	92	93	94	95	96	97	98	99	100

II Choose 2 numbers from the hundred chart that you did **not** color. For each number, write a short word problem with that number as the answer.

1. _____

   _____

2. _____

   _____

I Have, Who Has?: Math • 1–2 © 2007 Creative Teaching Press

Blank Card Template

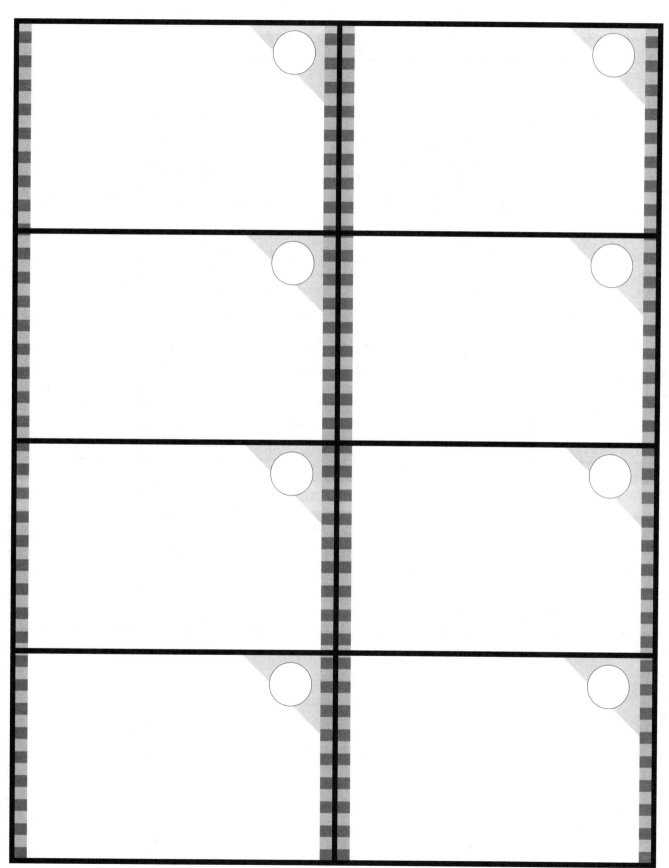

Reproducible Enrichment Activity Pages

1	2	3	4	5	6	7	8	9	10
11	12	13	14	15	16	17	18	19	20
21	22	23	24	25	26	27	28	29	30
31	32	33	34	35	36	37	38	39	40
41	42	43	44	45	46	47	48	49	50
51	52	53	54	55	56	57	58	59	60
61	62	63	64	65	66	67	68	69	70
71	72	73	74	75	76	77	78	79	80
81	82	83	84	85	86	87	88	89	90
91	92	93	94	95	96	97	98	99	100

I Have, Who Has? Math • 1–2 © 2007 Creative Teaching Press

*Start →							

*Start						
						*Finish

Answer Key

One More — Game A: Numbers < 100 (Page 11)

1	2	3	4	5	6	7	8	9	10
11	12	13	14	15	16	17	18	19	20
21	22	23	24	25	26	27	28	29	30
31	32	33	34	35	36	37	38	39	40
41	42	43	44	45	46	47	48	49	50
51	52	53	54	55	56	57	58	59	60
61	62	63	64	65	66	67	68	69	70
71	72	73	74	75	76	77	78	79	80
81	82	83	84	85	86	87	88	89	90
91	92	93	94	95	96	97	98	99	100

Answers will vary.

One Less — Game A: Numbers < 100 (Page 21)

1	2	3	4	5	6	7	8	9	10
11	12	13	14	15	16	17	18	19	20
21	22	23	24	25	26	27	28	29	30
31	32	33	34	35	36	37	38	39	40
41	42	43	44	45	46	47	48	49	50
51	52	53	54	55	56	57	58	59	60
61	62	63	64	65	66	67	68	69	70
71	72	73	74	75	76	77	78	79	80
81	82	83	84	85	86	87	88	89	90
91	92	93	94	95	96	97	98	99	100

Answers will vary.

One More — Game B: Numbers > 100 (Page 16)

*Start →	111	116	155	171	110	190	113
150	188	191	160	174	181	185	115
130	137	170	162	200	203	300	218
240	251	269	280	212	210	252	208

Answers will vary.

One Less — Game B: Numbers > 100 (Page 26)

*Start	101	149	154	249	265	302	400	*Finish
157	120	114	111	193	280	360	399	489
165	179	190	199	500	289	359	363	470
100	200	278	282	209	214	398	396	220
420	305	299	354	370	388	320	290	313
340	320	304	319	378	312	404	331	428

Answers will vary.

One More, One Less Review Game (Page 31)

*Start →	25	16	30	20	11	29	44
21	78	49	84	13	56	70	89
15	67	62	75	91	51	59	36
18	80	69	39	48	42	19	87

Answers will vary.

Two More, Five More Game: Numbers ≤ 50 (Page 36)

*Start	10	22	17	25	15	5	32
45	20	50	3	36	44	35	40
18	42	13	30	26	46	6	12
16	47	2	21	41	9	11	31

Answers will vary.

Two Less, Five Less Game: Numbers ≤ 50 (Page 41)

*Start	5	45	10	50	18	38	81
95	20	36	14	12	3	6	42
15	8	35	0	80	75	19	28
30	13	45	25	23	22	41	66
51	48	4	2	11	64	70	52
73	62	35	40	7	16	29	*Finish

Answers will vary.

Ten More — Game A: Numbers < 100 (Page 46)

1	2	3	4	5	6	7	8	9	10
11	12	13	14	15	16	17	18	19	20
21	22	23	24	25	26	27	28	29	30
31	32	33	34	35	36	37	38	39	40
41	42	43	44	45	46	47	48	49	50
51	52	53	54	55	56	57	58	59	60
61	62	63	64	65	66	67	68	69	70
71	72	73	74	75	76	77	78	79	80
81	82	83	84	85	86	87	88	89	90
91	92	93	94	95	96	97	98	99	100

Answers will vary.

Ten More — Game B: Numbers > 100 (Page 51)

*Start →	110	115	130	107	124	101	132
143	159	190	187	103	121	127	106
126	199	181	200	204	220	265	201
209	224	286	299	208	213	305	320

Answers will vary.

Ten Less — Game A: Numbers < 100 (Page 56)

1	2	3	4	5	6	7	8	9	10
11	12	13	14	15	16	17	18	19	20
21	22	23	24	25	26	27	28	29	30
31	32	33	34	35	36	37	38	39	40
41	42	43	44	45	46	47	48	49	50
51	52	53	54	55	56	57	58	59	60
61	62	63	64	65	66	67	68	69	70
71	72	73	74	75	76	77	78	79	80
81	82	83	84	85	86	87	88	89	90
91	92	93	94	95	96	97	98	99	100

Answers will vary.

Ten Less — Game B: Numbers > 100 (Page 61)

*Start	115	137	144	189	155	218	304	*Finish
101	127	134	143	150	105	281	291	281
105	115	189	107	270	205	283	194	201
107	119	150	111	265	209	212	227	199
111	131	200	255	200	190	104	202	380
106	146	108	103	129	160	121	306	303

Answers will vary.

Comparing Numbers Game (Page 66)

1	2	3	4	5	6	7	8	9	10
11	12	13	14	15	16	17	18	19	20
21	22	23	24	25	26	27	28	29	30
31	32	33	34	35	36	37	38	39	40
41	42	43	44	45	46	47	48	49	50
51	52	53	54	55	56	57	58	59	60
61	62	63	64	65	66	67	68	69	70
71	72	73	74	75	76	77	78	79	80
81	82	83	84	85	86	87	88	89	90
91	92	93	94	95	96	97	98	99	100

1. 68
2. 23
3. 94

Doubles and Doubles + 1 Game (Page 71)

*Start →	10	2	8	6	4	14	20
12	18	16	40	50	100	60	11
5	21	9	7	3	15	19	13
17	0 + 0	11 + 11	5 + 5	10 + 10	2 + 2	4 + 4	1 + 1

Answers will vary.

Addition — Game A: Two Terms and All Sums < 50 (Page 76)

1	2	3	4	5	6	7	8	9	10
11	12	13	14	15	16	17	18	19	20
21	22	23	24	25	26	27	28	29	30
31	32	33	34	35	36	37	38	39	40
41	42	43	44	45	46	47	48	49	50

Answers will vary.

Addition — Game B: Three Terms, Using Doubles, and All Sums < 100 (Page 81)

*Start →	3	15	30	23	20	13	14
5	29	11	1	17	44	63	50
69	6	4	12	16	18	40	60
51	43	85	31	7	25	35	37

Answers will vary.

Communtative Property of Addition Game (Page 86)

*Start	7 + 5	3 + 2	2 + 1	1 + 8	4 + 6	3 + 4	1 + 9
2 + 4	9 + 1	9 + 8	3 + 4	5 + 7	9 + 5	1 + 7	2 + 8
6 + 8	8 + 3	4 + 1	2 + 5	5 + 1	4 + 7	5 + 7	9 + 7
5 + 8	6 + 7	9 + 4	3 + 5	2 + 7	6 + 5	3 + 9	6 + 2
2 + 9	3 + 7	6 + 1	4 + 6	2 + 9	1 + 4	5 + 4	3 + 6
5 + 1	4 + 8	9 + 6	3 + 2	5 + 8	7 + 6	1 + 3	*Finish

Answers will vary.

Subtraction — Game A: Two Terms and All Differences < 50 (Page 91)

1	2	3	4	5	6	7	8	9	10
11	12	13	14	15	16	17	18	19	20
21	22	23	24	25	26	27	28	29	30
31	32	33	34	35	36	37	38	39	40
41	42	43	44	45	46	47	48	49	50

Answers will vary.

Subtraction — Game B:
Two Terms and All Differences < 100 (Page 96)

*Start →	1	5	18	20	10	17	30
3	14	23	44	29	2	74	50
39	34	9	13	38	40	60	63
51	84	79	59	81	31	69	78

Answers will vary.

Fact Families — Game A:
Identify the 2 Missing Subtraction Facts (Page 101)

*Start	8 − 3 = 5 8 − 5 = 3	4 − 1 = 3 4 − 3 = 1	7 − 3 = 4 7 − 4 = 3	7 − 1 = 6 7 − 6 = 1	9 − 3 = 6 9 − 6 = 3
3 − 1 = 2 3 − 2 = 1	6 − 2 = 4 6 − 4 = 2	9 − 2 = 7 9 − 7 = 2	11 − 2 = 9 11 − 9 = 2	7 − 2 = 5 7 − 5 = 2	5 − 1 = 4 5 − 4 = 1
13 − 3 = 10 13 − 10 = 3	11 − 5 = 6 11 − 6 = 5	11 − 3 = 8 11 − 8 = 3	8 − 1 = 7 8 − 7 = 1	9 − 1 = 8 9 − 8 = 1	5 − 2 = 3 5 − 3 = 2
15 − 5 = 10 15 − 10 = 5	9 − 4 = 5 9 − 5 = 4	12 − 2 = 10 12 − 10 = 2	6 − 5 = 1 6 − 1 = 5	10 − 3 = 7 10 − 7 = 3	9 − 3 = 6 9 − 6 = 3
10 − 4 = 6 10 − 6 = 4	12 − 5 = 7 12 − 7 = 5	9 − 3 = 6 9 − 6 = 3	12 − 3 = 9 12 − 9 = 3	7 − 2 = 5 7 − 5 = 2	10 − 1 = 9 10 − 9 = 1
13 − 5 = 8 13 − 8 = 5	11 − 4 = 7 11 − 7 = 4	14 − 5 = 9 14 − 9 = 5	10 − 2 = 8 10 − 8 = 2	15 − 6 = 9 15 − 9 = 6	*Finish
13 − 6 = 7 13 − 7 = 6	12 − 4 = 8 12 − 8 = 4	13 − 6 = 7 13 − 7 = 6	12 − 4 = 8 12 − 8 = 4	13 − 4 = 9 13 − 9 = 4	14 − 6 = 8 14 − 8 = 6

Answers will vary.

Fact Families — Game B:
Identify the 2 Missing Addition Facts (Page 106)

*Start	1 + 2 = 3 2 + 1 = 3	2 + 4 = 6 4 + 2 = 6	3 + 5 = 8 5 + 3 = 8	1 + 5 = 6 5 + 1 = 6	2 + 7 = 9 7 + 2 = 9
4 + 6 = 10 6 + 4 = 10	5 + 4 = 9 4 + 5 = 9	1 + 4 = 5 4 + 1 = 5	2 + 5 = 7 5 + 2 = 7	1 + 3 = 4 3 + 1 = 4	3 + 8 = 11 8 + 3 = 11
1 + 6 = 7 6 + 1 = 7	3 + 7 = 10 7 + 3 = 10	2 + 6 = 8 6 + 2 = 8	7 + 2 = 9 2 + 7 = 9	3 + 9 = 12 9 + 3 = 12	1 + 7 = 8 7 + 1 = 8
2 + 9 = 11 9 + 2 = 11	7 + 5 = 12 5 + 7 = 12	4 + 5 = 9 5 + 4 = 9	5 + 8 = 13 8 + 5 = 13	6 + 9 = 15 9 + 6 = 15	4 + 7 = 11 7 + 4 = 11
3 + 4 = 7 4 + 3 = 7	1 + 8 = 9 8 + 1 = 9	6 + 7 = 13 7 + 6 = 13	5 + 6 = 11 6 + 5 = 11	7 + 8 = 15 8 + 7 = 15	5 + 10 = 15 10 + 5 = 15
4 + 9 = 13 9 + 4 = 13	2 + 10 = 12 10 + 2 = 12	2 + 3 = 5 3 + 2 = 5	4 + 8 = 12 8 + 4 = 12	2 + 3 = 5 3 + 2 = 5	6 + 7 = 13 7 + 6 = 13
4 + 10 = 14 10 + 4 = 14	1 + 9 = 10 9 + 1 = 10	3 + 10 = 13 10 + 3 = 13	6 + 10 = 16 10 + 6 = 16	5 + 8 = 13 8 + 5 = 13	4 + 5 = 9 5 + 4 = 9
3 + 8 = 11 8 + 3 = 11	3 + 5 = 8 5 + 3 = 8	2 + 8 = 10 8 + 2 = 10	3 + 6 = 9 6 + 3 = 9	4 + 6 = 10 6 + 4 = 10	*Finish

Answers will vary.

Multiplication: Making Groups Game (Page 111)

*Start →	7	13	26	39	500	2	10
4	20	50	100	60	80	6	3
30	75	90	15	25	24	14	1
5	8	40	9	12	22	16	18

1. 100	6. 80
2. 20	7. 5
3. 90	8. 75
4. 3	9. 25
5. 8	10. 4

Patterns — Game A: Extend the Pattern (Page 116)

1	2	3	4	5	6	7	8	9	10
11	12	13	14	15	16	17	18	19	20
21	22	23	24	25	26	27	28	29	30
31	32	33	34	35	36	37	38	39	40
41	42	43	44	45	46	47	48	49	50
51	52	53	54	55	56	57	58	59	60
61	62	63	64	65	66	67	68	69	70
71	72	73	74	75	76	77	78	79	80
81	82	83	84	85	86	87	88	89	90
91	92	93	94	95	96	97	98	99	100

Answers will vary.

Patterns — Game B: What Is Missing? (Page 121)

1	2	3	4	5	6	7	8	9	10
11	12	13	14	15	16	17	18	19	20
21	22	23	24	25	26	27	28	29	30
31	32	33	34	35	36	37	38	39	40
41	42	43	44	45	46	47	48	49	50
51	52	53	54	55	56	57	58	59	60
61	62	63	64	65	66	67	68	69	70
71	72	73	74	75	76	77	78	79	80
81	82	83	84	85	86	87	88	89	90
91	92	93	94	95	96	97	98	99	100

Answers will vary.

Guess My Number: Clues with Even/Odd, </>, and Place Value Game (Page 126)

1	2	3	4	5	6	7	8	9	10
11	12	13	14	15	16	17	18	19	20
21	22	23	24	25	26	27	28	29	30
31	32	33	34	35	36	37	38	39	40
41	42	43	44	45	46	47	48	49	50
51	52	53	54	55	56	57	58	59	60
61	62	63	64	65	66	67	68	69	70
71	72	73	74	75	76	77	78	79	80
81	82	83	84	85	86	87	88	89	90
91	92	93	94	95	96	97	98	99	100

Answers will vary.

Place Value — Game A: Combine Tens and Ones into a Number (Page 131)

1	2	3	4	5	6	7	8	9	10
11	12	13	14	15	16	17	18	19	20
21	22	23	24	25	26	27	28	29	30
31	32	33	34	35	36	37	38	39	40
41	42	43	44	45	46	47	48	49	50
51	52	53	54	55	56	57	58	59	60
61	62	63	64	65	66	67	68	69	70
71	72	73	74	75	76	77	78	79	80
81	82	83	84	85	86	87	88	89	90
91	92	93	94	95	96	97	98	99	100

Answers will vary.

Place Value — Game B: Adding Tens and Ones (Page 136)

*Start	7 tens 6 ones	4 tens 1 one	7 tens 9 ones
2 tens 6 ones	9 tens 9 ones	3 tens 0 ones	4 tens 5 ones
2 tens 0 ones	7 tens 4 ones	2 tens 5 ones	1 ten 9 ones
7 tens 7 ones	5 tens 2 ones	9 tens 4 ones	5 tens 4 ones
2 tens 4 ones	3 tens 4 ones	4 tens 7 ones	4 tens 5 ones
6 tens 4 ones	1 ten 7 ones	7 tens 0 ones	8 tens 1 one
3 tens 0 ones	2 tens 1 one	2 tens 2 ones	1 ten 4 ones
1 ten 2 ones	5 tens 5 ones	7 tens 2 ones	9 tens 7 ones
4 tens 6 ones	5 tens 7 ones	5 tens 0 ones	3 tens 2 ones
1 ten 1 one	7 tens 5 ones	9 tens 2 ones	*Finish

Column A: 9 tens 9 ones
Column C: 9 tens 9 ones

Place Value — Game C:
Practice on the Hundred Chart (Page 141)

1	2	3	4	5	6	7	8	9	10
11	12	13	14	15	16	17	18	19	20
21	22	23	24	25	26	27	28	29	30
31	32	33	34	35	36	37	38	39	40
41	42	43	44	45	46	47	48	49	50
51	52	53	54	55	56	57	58	59	60
61	62	63	64	65	66	67	68	69	70
71	72	73	74	75	76	77	78	79	80
81	82	83	84	85	86	87	88	89	90
91	92	93	94	95	96	97	98	99	100

Answers will vary.

Place Value — Game D: Regrouping (Page 146)

1	2	3	4	5	6	7	8	9	10
11	12	13	14	15	16	17	18	19	20
21	22	23	24	25	26	27	28	29	30
31	32	33	34	35	36	37	38	39	40
41	42	43	44	45	46	47	48	49	50
51	52	53	54	55	56	57	58	59	60
61	62	63	64	65	66	67	68	69	70
71	72	73	74	75	76	77	78	79	80
81	82	83	84	85	86	87	88	89	90
91	92	93	94	95	96	97	98	99	100

1. 100
2. 42
3. 81
4. 50

Time — Game A: Basic Concepts, ½ Hour, Hour,
and Elapsed Time to ½ Hour and Hour (Page 151)

*Start	long hand	11:00	7:00	3:30	1:30
minute hand	short hand	2:00	10:00	5:30	9:30
hour hand	60 minutes	6:30	4:30	7:30	10:30
24 hours	30 minutes	3:00	2:30	8:30	2:00
a.m.	p.m.	5:00	12:00	4:00	12:00
7:30	8:00	11:00	9:00	1:00	3:30
2:30	3:00	5:00	6:00	12:30	1:30
4:30	6:30	2:00	11:00	11:30	*Finish

Answers will vary.

Time — Game B: ¼ Hour, ½ Hour, ¾ Hour,
and Hour with Elapsed Time (Page 156)

*Start →	4:30	12:00	8:15
5:45	1:00	12:30	2:00
10:30	5:15	2:45	3:45
11:15	3:15	6:45	7:45
10:15	4:45	6:15	1:30
9:30	12:45	10:00	4:00
7:00	8:45	11:45	7:15
4:15	1:15	3:00	7:30

Answers will vary.

Time — Game C: Calendar (Page 161)

*Start	4 seasons	Sunday	Tuesday	2nd	30th
7 days	12 months	Wednesday	Thursday	12th	24th
10th	Friday	Saturday	October	4th	26th
Monday	Tuesday	February	November	1st	29th
Thursday	June	August	April	15th	10th
Friday	Wednesday	May	September	13th	20th
December	March	January	November	3rd	22nd
July	October	31st	8th	11th	*Finish

1. Monday; Tuesday; Wednesday; Thursday; Friday; Saturday; Sunday
2. 7; 14
3. 5
4. 5
5. 31st

Money — Game A: Coin Identification, Values, and Counting Money Under $1.00 (Page 167)

*Start	55¢	10¢	100¢	1¢	50¢
penny	35¢	25¢	dollar	2 nickels	5¢
nickel	dime	quarter	half dollar	10 dimes	5 nickels
75¢	30¢	2 dimes and 1 nickel	25 pennies	5 dimes	4 quarters
17¢	28¢	60¢	5 dollars	2 quarters	2 half dollars
51¢	35¢	38¢	79¢	40¢	27¢
80¢	75¢	17¢	85¢	99¢	65¢
84¢	44¢	15¢	45¢	22¢	*Finish

Answers will vary.

Money — Game B: Counting Money with Coins and Dollars (Page 172)

*Start →	$1.50	$1.20	$1.02
$2.00	$1.30	$1.15	$1.75
$1.25	$1.70	$1.10	$1.05
$1.01	$1.51	$1.60	$1.55
$1.35	$1.45	$2.50	$2.40
$2.75	$2.25	$1.26	$1.11
$1.09	$1.65	$1.80	$1.85
$1.58	$1.95	$1.00	$1.90

Answers will vary.

Units of Length, Capacity, Weight, and Time Game (Page 177)

*Start	length	capacity	time	weight	2 cups	*Finish
2 pints	24 inches	3 feet	36 inches	12 inches	pint	quart
2 cups	9 feet	365 days	hour	foot	minute	60 seconds
2 quarts	4 quarts	52 weeks	7 days	6 inches	year	3 feet
40 quarts	8 pints	15 minutes	45 minutes	day	week	4 quarts
16 ounces	60 seconds	30 minutes	12 inches	60 minutes	365 days	2 pints

1. d
2. a
3. f
4. b
5. c
6. e
7. g

Data Analysis —Game A: Bar and Pie Graphs (Page 182)

*Start	pie graph	title	5 people	mint chip
"My Normal Weekend Day"	bar graph	rats and hamsters	rabbit	vanilla and strawberry
horizontal bars	vertical bars	6 people	pie graph	2 people
25 people	23 people	0 people	to show change over time	4 hours
24 hours	sleeping	guinea pig	doing chores and eating	sleeping
to show the parts of a whole	to compare different information	dog	5 hours	no people
8 hours	22 hours	6 hours	8 hours	rabbit
11 hours	9 hours	vanilla and strawberry	mint chip	5 people
11 people	7 people	15 people	1 hour	*Finish

1. b
2. c
3. a

Data Analysis — Game B: Reading a Table (Page 188)

*Start →	8	12	13
11	21	17	14
7	6	36	19
16	10	18	15
22	24	30	28
26	20	27	35
33	23	25	31
34	40	38	44

Answers will vary.

Word Problems Game (Page 194)

1	2	3	4	5	6	7	8	9	10
11	12	13	14	15	16	17	18	19	20
21	22	23	24	25	26	27	28	29	30
31	32	33	34	35	36	37	38	39	40
41	42	43	44	45	46	47	48	49	50
51	52	53	54	55	56	57	58	59	60
61	62	63	64	65	66	67	68	69	70
71	72	73	74	75	76	77	78	79	80
81	82	83	84	85	86	87	88	89	90
91	92	93	94	95	96	97	98	99	100

Answers will vary.

Notes

Notes